How to Have Family Prayers

BOOKS BY ROSALIND RINKER . . .

Communicating Love Through Prayer

The Open Heart

Prayer: Conversing With God

Praying Together

Who Is This Man?

Within the Circle

The Years That Count

You Can Witness With Confidence

Sharing God's Love (co-author)

How to Have Family Prayers

Rosalind Rinker

OF THE ZONDERVAN CORPORATION | GRAND RAPIDS, MICHIGAN 49506

Illustrations by Walter Kerr

How to Have Family Prayers

Third printing November 1977

Library of Congress Cataloging in Publication Data

Rinker, Rosalind.
How to have family prayers.
Bibliography: p.
1. Family—Religious life. 2. Family—Prayer-books and devotions—English. I. Title.
BV4526.2.R56 248'.8 76-56797

Cloth: ISBN 0-310-32160-3
Paper: ISBN 0-310-32161-1

Printed in the United States of America

This book
is dedicated to
YOUNG PARENTS
who care enough to give
their children memories of
the family praying together.

Contents

Part I — For Parents

Chapter 1 Does My Daddy Love Me? *13*
Chapter 2 The Miracle of Giving and Receiving Love *19*
Chapter 3 What Does Your Family Need? *25*
Chapter 4 The Benefits of Prayer and Meditation *35*
Chapter 5 Being a Member of the Family *41*
Chapter 6 Questions People Ask Me *51*

Part II — For Parents and Children

Chapter 7 The Presence of God *69*
Chapter 8 The Miracle of Thankfulness *77*
Chapter 9 The Healing of Confession *85*
Chapter 10 Praying for Others *95*

Part III — 30 Days of Daily Devotions

First Week The Person of Jesus Christ *107*
Second Week What Jesus Said About Himself *123*
Third Week Precious Promises from God *139*
Fourth Week Praying Through the Psalms *155*

Chapter Notes *165*
Bibliography *167*

Acknowledgments

My thanks to ten of my good friends who assisted in a survey on family prayers: Virginia Conard, Dorothy Busse, Helen Classen, Ina Gustin, Grace McCoy, Lorraine Murphy, Len Sehested, Suzanne Varn, Ruth Westervelt, Corinne Wong. Also to my secretary Martha Burger for her faithful help on the manuscript, and to Elaine Reedy for her personal support and prayers. My thanks to the Friday morning prayer group of St. James Episcopal Church, Newport Beach, California. And my special thanks to Rhea Zakish for the sessions together on content, and to Robert DeVries and Judy Markham, my beloved friends and editors who love me and believe in me.

Foreword

My recognition of the need for a book of this kind came out of numerous speaking engagements which took me into all kinds of homes, both here in the States and on our military bases abroad. The fast pace of today's living (plus the ever-present TV) cuts communication down to almost nil, until there is seldom time for the family to eat together, let alone pray together.

As a counselor of college students (for fourteen years with Inter-Varsity Christian Fellowship), I found that the students who responded to the call of Jesus were those who came from a home background of love, prayer, and church. Those who came from broken and bitter homes felt that if there was a God, He couldn't possibly be interested in them.

What kind of a heritage are you giving your children?

What will they remember about home in later years? Going to church? Being sent to Sunday school while parents stayed home? Will they remember conversations about trust in God and where stories of answered prayer were told? Will they remember that real help comes by loving and by praying with and for one another?

Will you give your children the heritage of remembering

father at prayer? Or mother praying for each child by name?

Prayer is communication on the highest level. Communication is being aware of the other person, of his character, and of his intentions toward you. Communication is listening and responding to what he says or what he doesn't say.

Prayer is a way of sharing and does make one vulnerable, but to be vulnerable means to be loved. Through prayer we learn how to open our hearts and say in words, as well as actions, what is in our hearts and minds.

ROSALIND RINKER

Part I
For Parents

"Father, Lord of heaven and earth,
to you I offer praise;
For what you have hidden from the
learned and the clever
You have revealed to the merest children."

— Matthew 11:25, NAB

1 *Does My Daddy Love Me?*

This book comes directly as a result of a visit to Europe in the fall of 1975 when I was invited to visit our U.S.A. military bases under NATO and be the speaker for their PWOC (Protestant Women of the Chapel) fall rallies. I was gone forty-five days and visited fifteen military bases in Norway, Belgium, Germany, and Italy.

The PWOC rallies were carefully planned and well organized, with good programing, original decorations, and eager, expectant women. I've been speaking to military personnel for more than ten years and find them very receptive. This may be because orders to move come about every three years, and this kind of displacement for a family creates its own problems.[1]

These rallies were held on a Saturday, with cars and buses of women coming from nearby bases. On the Friday night before the rally there was a meeting for men and women on the base, preceded by a potluck supper. These were well attended and were usually held in the gymnasiums of American schools. And the whole family came!

As the remains of the meal were being cleared away, I noticed several people herding the children out of the room. In dismay I asked, "Where are you taking them?" I've found that children learn to pray quicker than adults and usually teach their parents how to pray.

I was told that there was a thirty-minute Walt Disney film ready for them in the next room. Immediately I went to the chaplain in charge and asked if the children could please remain for the meeting. I explained that I am an informal speaker with a simple message which children love. Would he give it a try? Then we would excuse the children to see their film while the adults had a question-and-answer period.

Time after time it happened just like that. Mary Virginia Parrish, the dear friend who traveled with me, was excellent with the children; she got them up in front facing their parents and taught them action songs and soon had involved their parents also. By the time I took over, there was a warm, informal atmosphere prevailing.

Then I presented the need for praying together as a family and how to do it. And we did it. Right there.

And here's what happened.

I was ready to leave a certain base in Italy, when a little woman came up and put her arms around me.

"Oh, thank you, Ros, for coming! You were an answer to my prayers."

"Well, it's like this. For the last three months I've been telling my husband it was time to start having family prayers, and he would say, 'Well, go ahead.' I would tell him that the *father* must take the lead, and he would counter with, 'I don't know what to do,' and so nothing was done. In desperation, I began to pray that God would somehow, some way, send us some help. And then you came and taught us!

"Did you see what happened to us last night at your meeting? When you asked families to pull their chairs into a circle? We were right on the front row."

I remembered seeing a family all in a huddle hugging each other. It was this family.

I had asked the families to sit in a circle and take hands. Then the parents were to start, saying to each child, "God loves you (John), and your mommie loves you." Or, "God loves you (Mary), and your daddy loves you, too."

In this family, the mother took the lead, starting with her oldest, a son of eleven.

"Ray, God loves you, and your mommie loves you." He looked up at her with his big, brown eyes, which quickly filled with overflowing tears, and said, as he looked over at his father, "But does my daddy love me?"

Of course daddy loved him, but he had never said it in words . . . until this moment, and then he gathered Ray into his arms and they cried together. The two little girls got into the act, and so did the mother.

But does my daddy love me? Does your child know he is loved? Have you ever told him? Or do you think he is too old now? Just giving *things* is not enough — not enough for you or me, or for anybody.

Love does not sit in a corner. Love acts and love speaks. We want both action and words. We *need* both. Without them we are impoverished and sometimes ill. Parents hold in their hands the maturity of their children as well as their physical well-being, and to withhold love from them is to stunt their growth. By withholding love from our children, we are preventing their personalities from maturing normally.

The time to start family prayers is when the children are small, for then their problems are fewer and their faith is greater. Their sense of Jesus' presence is greater, their little hearts are open, and they are not afraid. If you wait until they are in their early teens, the door may be closed. Then they are already living their own lives and are embarrassed to pray in front of you, their parents. They have nothing to say; communication is cut off. It is probably too late.

So, no matter how unsure you (father or mother) are of yourself, just step out on faith — like Peter did when he walked on the waves — and get started. Your children will help you. God Himself will be with you to help you.

The seeds which you sow now will grow into love, understanding, communication, and security. Otherwise, without a prayer life in your family, you will be reaping a harvest of quiet resentment, secrecy, and dishonesty with no communication.

Which will it be?

For Thought and Discussion

1. What kinds of problems would be created by moving a family every three years?
2. How would you handle those problems?
3. Why do children learn to pray quicker than adults?
4. What door was opened for the family in Italy? Why was it closed before that?
5. What good qualities result from having family prayers?

2 *The Miracle of Giving and Receiving Love*

The purpose of this book is to help parents master a few simple steps which will assist in beginning family prayers, with a view to bringing the maximum appreciation, love, and understanding to each member.

Any person who has difficulty in expressing or giving love, or receiving it, can probably trace the source of that abnormality back to some specific childhood experience.

I remember the first time I ever heard anyone say they did not believe God loved them. I was being driven to one of my speaking engagements, and there were three strangers in the back seat of the car in which I was riding. During the ride, one of them said bitterly, "I don't believe God loves me at all!" When I asked her why she thought that, she only repeated it more emphatically without any explanation. Later, one of the women told me that this person had grown up in a very unhappy home where the children were neither wanted nor loved.

But I assure you, there is healing for every painful childhood memory *for those who desire it.*

While taking part in a *Faith At Work* conference in Georgia several years ago, I led a workshop on prayer and gave the group one of my *creative meditations* to help them realize God's presence and love. They were asked to close their eyes and try to live in the story of Jesus receiving the children, as I told it (Mark 10:13-16).

As soon as the session was over, a distraught woman cornered me. "You want me to be a little child again? Well, that has thrown me into terrible confusion! That was the unhappiest time of my whole life!"

"Would you like to tell me about it?" I asked. "I'm sure God has an answer for you."

She proceeded to tell me that when she was very young, an only child, both parents had been killed in an automobile accident. The courts had given her into custody of two old-maid aunts who knew nothing about bringing up a little girl. Whippings and discipline without love were her constant lot. She was compelled to wear clothes no other little girls wore, and so on. She ran away from home, but the police brought her back. This resulted in more whippings. . . . So she cried herself to sleep night after night, blaming God for taking her mother away from her.

As she spoke, I trusted the wisdom of the Holy Spirit to show me what to do next, and He did.

"My dear, that little girl within you needs the healing touch of Jesus' hands. Sit down here, and I'll pray for you." As I laid hands on her, words of love, words of healing were given to me as I prayed for her; she got up, thanked me, and left.

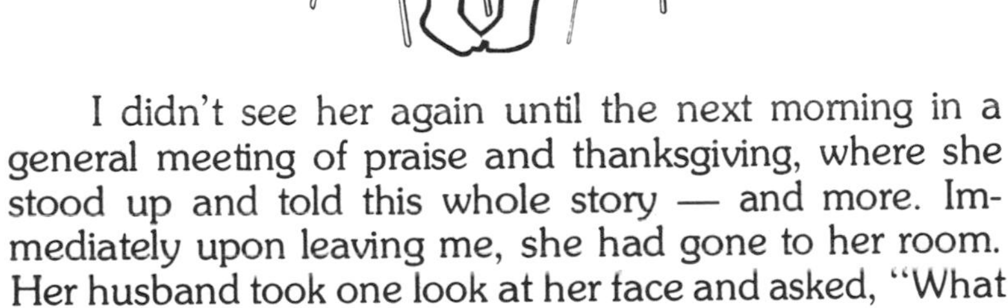

I didn't see her again until the next morning in a general meeting of praise and thanksgiving, where she stood up and told this whole story — and more. Immediately upon leaving me, she had gone to her room. Her husband took one look at her face and asked, "What happened to you?"

"I was prayed for, and Jesus healed the little girl inside me." And she told him how it had happened.

Then it was his turn, for he needed such a healing. She told him to sit down, and she prayed for him — and Jesus healed the little boy inside that grown man, healed all the hurt places which had been hidden for so many years.

Actually, this was the beginning of a new ministry, or gift of the Spirit given to me, which has now come to be known as the *healing of memories.*

The Prayer of Healing

As parents, if you are unable to give love to each other

or to your children (or are unable to receive love), spend some quiet times together in meditation and confession and receive the healing touch of Jesus. If you are unable to do this for yourself or each other, pray that God will direct you to someone who has been given this ministry.

When you have experienced this healing yourself, God will enable you to give healing to your children in their times of trauma or pain, so that these painful experiences will not be built up and stored away to quietly plague them the rest of their lives.

This is what prayer is all about.

Prayer is a ministry of love and healing to your family.

Prayer is a conversation between people who love each other: releasing, refreshing, restoring, and healing.

The Source of Love

In the first chapter, it was the simplicity of pronouncing words of love which drew that family together on the military base in Italy — when mother first said, "Ray, God loves you, and your mommie loves you."

There is only one way to have a successful family life: *Love one another as I have loved you.* This sounds impossible, I know, but Jesus said it. Jesus makes it possible when we pray from our hearts.

During the past ten years I've observed amazing things happen when people pray together. They love one another! It happens over and over.

We are drawn together by our mutual needs and common weaknesses. As we call on God who is always near us, who loves us, who forgives us, who comforts us, and who heals us . . . He gives us Himself! So, His presence with us becomes our first answer to prayer. Our hearts are moved toward Him and toward each other. God loves us, and we love each other. Such love is a miracle!

The importance of being loved is second only to the importance of giving love. It is as essential to love someone as it is to be loved. They are two sides to one coin.

As parents, you may feel there already is love in your family, and I'm sure there must be some or you would not be together. But not all love can communicate effectively. And because all love has its source in God Himself, we need to make a definite point of reinforcing our human love with God's love.

The Greek language, from which our New Testament Scriptures were translated, has three words for our one English word *love.*

Philos: brotherly love
Eros: sexual love
Agape: God's love

With the reinforcement of God's love (*agape*) joined to our brotherly love *(philos),* communication becomes a pleasure and a joy. For prayer is a love-language of the heart.

First, we must repeat the motive for family prayers so it is clear in our thinking: We want to start having family prayers in order to bring the maximum appreciation, love, and understanding to each family member.

Next, we need to plan for the time, the place, and the procedure. After that, the loving words will come — and the loving actions too — for God is with us and for us, and He loves us eternally.

Talking to God is prayer.

Praying together as a family unit opens the door to loving one another.

When I have prayed with you, I understand you better. I even understand myself better.

When you have prayed with me, you understand me better. You even understand yourself better.

Thus love is nourished and begins to flourish.

This is the first lesson in prayer: to be willing to give and receive love in your family prayer time.

Morton T. Kelsey has said:

> One must experience love to know it. And if he would know God, he had best seek until he finds Him, because a man can never know or love God until he has known love from and to his brother. . . .
>
> It is often difficult for us to express our love to those who are nearest to us . . . our families. It is strange how we let our pride and hurtness, our ideas and feelings out of the past, keep us from expressing love where it should be most expected and is most needed. . . . Indeed, until one can give love and understanding and appreciation without any strings attached, without expecting anything in return, he is only part of the whole person he was intended to be. No matter how physically or intellectually grown up, he is still simply an immature emotional child.[1]

For Thought and Discussion

1. What is the purpose of this book?
2. Why is it often difficult to express love to those nearest us?
3. Discuss the subject of inability to receive love — its source, its results, its healing.
4. Share what you know about the *healing of memories.*
5. How does praying as a family open the door to God's love *(agape)?* What does it bring to the members of the family?
6. Name other things prayer does.

3 *What Does Your Family Need?*

Larry Christenson, a Lutheran pastor, has written several helpful books on family life. He is in demand as a teacher and counselor for family conferences and has spoken to thousands of couples who are desperately searching for a better family life. In his small booklet *Which Way the Family?*, he writes:

> *Mothers* tearfully relate the lies and deceptions which come to light with a teenage daughter, or the rebellion of a son seemingly against every kind of adult authority.
>
> *Fathers* shake their heads in puzzlement over the sweet daughter who almost overnight sheds her girlhood innocence for suggestive dress, stringy hair, hard-looking companions and often drugs.
>
> *Parents* are in bewilderment at the unreasonable attitudes and demands of seven and eight-year-old children — and usually give in to them.
>
> *Wives* complain about the husband who never has time to spend with the family, yet expects her to keep the house and children running like a precision clock.
>
> *Husbands* wonder why they should have to battle the world

> for a living ten or twelve hours a day, then come home and open the door to the clamor of still more problems. The husband . . . is frustrated; the wife . . . nags, and the children are sullen or withdrawn. Yet behind all these reactions stands a single plea: *What can we do?*[1]

In answer to the above question — What can we do to make family life work better? — Pastor Christenson gives a few suggestions:

> 1. That the fathers (and mothers, my addition) set the course in establishing and maintaining the direction.
> 2. That religious training through family prayers should be provided by the parents, and not left entirely to the church.
> 3. That the father (and mother, my addition) should be under the loving authority of God and responsible to Him in all affairs. For instance, if the father is not responsible to God in his finances, should he be surprised if his children's financial affairs get fouled up? Our sins and failures (unapparent to the world) often show up in our children.[2]

I wouldn't be so dogmatic as to insist that the only remedy for family disunity lies in regular family prayers, but I am bold to state (because of long experience in teaching prayer workshops) that the family altar provides the right place to build harmony and forgiveness which in turn produce understanding and appreciation. These are the goals we need to keep in mind for wholeness and health both for children and for parents. Actually these are God's gifts to us as we meet together in His presence.

Why is it so difficult to have family prayers?

In a survey of Christian homes, I found that in today's world only a few have daily family prayers. Most have grace at the table and some kind of bedtime prayer or story in the children's rooms.

Here is a list of the difficulties which were given as reasons for not having a prayer time:

Nobody eats at the same time.
Extracurricular activities.
We don't know how.
We don't have time.
We aren't trained to do this.
I'm afraid I'd fall flat on my face.
I don't know how to pray.
I never pray aloud.
I can't pray as well as others do.
I don't know how to get started.
Let my wife do it.
I'd be embarrassed and so would the children.

These objections are nothing but excuses. In fact, they are fears, which in turn are based on destructive tensions. Show me a family who cannot pray together,

and I'll show you a family who cannot "talk it out" either. Those three little words are a powerful key to draining off tension, and when "talking it out" becomes "praying it out," we begin turning our liabilities into assets.

The secret to minimizing destructive tensions in family life is to "talk it out." Remember that old gospel song — "Just a little talk with Jesus makes it right — all right"?

Family tensions need action patterns which can be put into words and into daily habits which develop and build strength. This is where family prayer comes into the picture.

How to Do It

1. *Table grace:* We have a thanksgiving conversation with God. Everyone gives thanks for at least one thing, ending with someone giving a sentence of thanks for the food.

2. *We then learn more:* We pray for ourselves and ask for what we need, while others voice audible agreement and give thanks. (This could come after the meal when we are comfortable with #1.)

3. *And more:* We learn how to say "I love you," and "I'm sorry," and "Please forgive me." In this loving atmosphere we begin to feel the acceptance we need. This can be done at the table any time it is needed.

4. *And then:* We learn how to pray for friends and loved ones. We learn just what to ask for so God's purposes can be worked out through us and in them.

Exercise your faith

You parents should begin by affirming the truth within yourself, and soon you will be saying it to each other:

"I believe we can do this in our family."
"We need to do this together."
"I believe we can do it."
"We *can* do it with God's help."
"Thank You, Jesus, for helping our unbelief."

What is faith?

Faith is looking at a situation and visualizing it, seeing it as it is going to be when God changes it. Seeing your family doing this together before it happens — that's faith. Giving God thanks before it happens — that's faith.

> "Thank You, Lord, for helping me face my fears."

Finding and Facing Objections

In Part II we will go into more detail on "how to do it," but right now we should lay to rest some of the very real fears (excuses) we have already mentioned so that confidence and faith may continue to develop.

1. *I'm not worthy.*

Many of you have already identified with the father in chapter one who "passed the buck" to his wife by saying, "Well, you do it." Whoever you are, I want to assure you that no one ever feels competent or worthy to have family prayers — so join the crowd.

Talking to God as a family opens the door to loving one another, for God is love, and He is there when you call on His name. We do not talk to an absent person, but to One who is always present, One who accepts us just as we are.

2. *I don't know how to start.*

If you could listen in to a family praying together, you would exclaim, "Is that all you do? Our family could do that!" Of course you can do it, with both parents taking turns as the leader.

a. You can get a good start by using Part III, a thirty-day devotional plan written out in detail.

b. You can carefully read about the four steps of prayer in Part II.

c. You can send for a Rinker cassette, *When the Family Prays Together,* and let your whole family listen to it.[3]

3. *We don't have time.*

In two to five minutes you can have short family prayers every day and start the day with God — with love and with confidence. This takes basic training in honesty and being willing to say it like it is, not mumbling set prayers. This you can do, too, if you only believe you can (with the help of God).

One mother I know, when time is short, gathers her little flock together right at the front door — coats and books and all — and prays: "Lord Jesus, You are here with us now, and You will be with Donnie, Jimmie, and Bonnie all day long. Help them remember to call on You when they need You. Thank You, Jesus. Amen." And if she forgets, they remind her!

4. *I'm not a praying man.*

All Jesus asks is that you move into a Father/son relationship with Him and become like a little child. That little child in your heart — he's there — let him speak to Jesus in simple everyday language. Then be willing to learn from your children. Once you make up your mind, God will assist you, and you will find that it isn't hard.

Let's face it, this is an emotional problem related to your pride. Is it worth it? Why not try it for the sake of your children?

5. *What about flowery words?*

Never mind about flowery words. We are not heard for our much speaking nor for our many fine words. God cannot be manipulated by words or methods or techniques. He is always moving toward us in love. In God's presence, the words will come when they are needed.

Freedom from Fear

"For God did not give us a spirit of timidity, but a spirit of power, of love and of self-discipline" (2 Tim. 1:7 NIV).

Do not accept the spirit of fear or timidity as exposed in any of the above excuses, for it is not from God, but from the enemy of God — Satan. Refuse it. Confess it. Give thanks for the positive gift from God, the gift of faith.

Giving thanks signifies a gift has been received.

The Family Altar

The family altar is a place where we can forgive and be forgiven. Where we can pray about not being selfish, or proud, or mean. Where we can show love for one another without being embarrassed. Where we can pray for our sick friends and relatives.

The family altar is a place where God hears and answers our prayers.

The family altar is a place where the risen Lord Jesus meets us, touches us, loves us, restores us, and sends us on our way rejoicing. And He does it by the work of His Holy Spirit in and through each one of us.

At the family altar, your family needs will begin to be supplied. Conscious and subconscious resentments and fears which have built up in both parents and children can be cleansed now, can be healed. Wounds made by thoughtless and harsh words, busy-ness, quarrels, or rejection can be healed there.

Admitting needs, confessing sins, and being prayed for by one another is the privilege of any family who will start a family altar.

* * *

> I like to compare prayer to the wind. You cannot actually *see* the wind, but you can see the results of it. . . . God has given us prayer that we might draw close to Him, that we might share our lives with Him, and that we might see the miracle of answered prayer each day of our lives. . . . How long has it been since you've seen a miracle in your life?[4]

For Thought and Discussion

1. What is the greatest need in your family?
2. How could Pastor Christenson's three suggestions change your family?
3. Read again the list of reasons (or excuses) for not

having family prayers and check those which sound like yours. Add any you have used or might use.
4. Close your eyes and visualize your family going through the four steps under *How to do it.*
5. What three things are suggested as a help in starting family prayers?
6. Finish this sentence with as many answers as you can: The family altar is a place where ____________________.

* * *

If you are in a class, divide into fours and pray for each other and for yourself, naming your fears. Expect a miracle. Take five minutes only.

If you are alone, tell God exactly what you can't do and why. He wants you to tell Him everything. Peace will come to you after you've prayed.

4 *The Benefits of Prayer and Meditation*

> The immediate purpose of praying is to grow in communion with our Triune God. This presupposes communication (transmission, receptivity and response between persons — not some sort of vague mystical silence) which involves speaking and listening to our Father so that we might *do His will* just as it is carried out in Heaven.[1]

The family altar can be in the kitchen, around the table, in the living room, or in the bedroom. It is a place where we can talk to God together and learn to listen to Him. It is also a time to love one another and express that love.

The benefits of praying together are legion. One of my early books is titled *Praying Together,* and it explores this life-changing subject at some length.[2]

Perhaps someone reading this will ask, "Why do we need to pray aloud? Why not just go into a room alone and practice TM? That seems to be the going thing to do."

I agree that just being quiet and apart for a short time in this restless, time-conscious world is like restoring one's sanity. Most Christians I know have a quiet time at the beginning of each day, a time they call "daily devotions." We ought to teach it and promote it more than we do — maybe someday I'll write a book on that subject!

When I first read the list of benefits which TM claims to give, I exclaimed, "Why, all of those things happen to the newborn child of God when the Holy Spirit takes over!" Here is a list taken from one of the TM books:

— increases physical and mental relaxation while raising alertness
— decreases blood pressure in the hypertense
— increases capacity for intimate contact with others
— decreases anxiety
— speeds up reaction time
— increases perceptual ability
— improves performance in school or on the job
— reduces use of alcohol, cigarettes, and non-prescribed drugs
— increases creativity and productivity
— increases personal satisfaction with life and work
— reduces depression and neuroticism [3]

* * *

There are differences between prayer and meditation, and there are differences between TM (Transcendental Meditation) and CM (Christian Meditation).

What Is Prayer?

Prayer is talking to God, audibly or silently. When there are no words, it is often called meditation. However, if you take time to read books on meditation, you will find that it is generally considered a higher form of communication with God than prayer and not as easily entered into because of distractions and lack of discipline.

All prayer presupposes there *is* Someone there — Someone who will open the door when we knock, who will give to us when we ask — the Lord our God, who in turn makes us aware of His presence.

What Is Meditation?

Evelyn Underhill writes, "Meditation is perhaps most simply defined as thinking in the Presence of God . . . and is the child of properly practised vocal prayer."[4]

M. V. Dunlop, another British writer, says, "True meditation is conscious communion with the most High God, or with Jesus Christ. It is quietly dwelling on some Word of Life from the Bible, until our consciousness realizes the Feeling for which the word stands."[5]

The Greek root for meditate is *meletao,* meaning "giving thought to, pondering, thinking about." The Psalms are full of the subject; and in the New Testament we are taught that when the mind is fully engaged with God, we are being prepared for action and for service.

Differences Between TM, CM, and Prayer

TM is something you do all by yourself without audible words. The teachers of this cult say that repeating your *mantra* silently helps to put your mind into neutral and supposedly opens you to experience ecstasy and reality. TM proponents claim their teachings are nonreligious, but actually they spring from Eastern religious thought in which there is no personal God.[6]

Christian meditation and prayer center our thoughts upon God who loves us or upon Jesus Christ to whom we belong as the branch belongs to the vine. The object of our

thoughts is a Person — whether we are alone or with others, whether we are silently meditating or sharing our praise and prayers aloud.

Two Kinds of Christians

At this point we need to distinguish between "nominal" Christians — who use the term as describing a nationality (almost) and who are not followers of Jesus — and "believing" Christians who enjoy faith in a personal God, resulting in a life-changing relationship with Him.

Organized religion, as we all know and deplore, has had a checkered, splintered history due to the shortcomings of human beings; but after all, organized religion is only the container, so to speak, for "God dwells within us." In John 17, Jesus prayed that we all might be one.

Thanks to the loving-kindness of our God, He has sent His own Spirit into the hearts of those who ask. They are referred to by St. Paul as the temple, the invisible temple of the living God.

Today God is doing a new thing; there is a fresh outpouring of His Spirit, which is seen as members of many denominations meet together as brothers and sisters to praise Him. You should become aware of what is taking place in this renewal movement.

I recently heard a friend proudly announce, when the subject of TM came up, "Well, I'll tell you what my *mantra* is — Jesus Christ!" (The TM people refuse to tell theirs.) I agreed with her, for Jesus is mine, too.

Did you ever hear of the *Jesus prayer?*

The *Jesus prayer* has come down to us from early Christianity, and numerous books and pamphlets have been printed on this subject.[7]

Lord Jesus Christ,
Son of God,
have mercy on me,
a sinner.

Actually, I use the Jesus prayer as the one repetitious and continuous prayer of my life. Repetitious, because I have learned that my subconscious mind is most deeply influenced by repetition. Continuous, because His name is powerful, and when I say His name the sense of His presence is with me and I find strength and reality for the current need.

In closing this chapter, may I remind you again of the purpose of this book: To help parents come to a strong belief in Christ in order that they might give their children the greatest heritage possible; that is, that they might establish a family altar, where by audibly praying together each member may receive the maximum appreciation, love, and understanding.

Refuse all negative thoughts of doubt, inferiority, or anxiety and be assured that affirmative prayer brings joyful, loving results. The following pages will give you clear simple instructions.

When we pray, when we say His name, we are consciously in the presence of our risen Lord Jesus, and He is the giver of all good gifts. He is waiting to pour them upon us in an ever-increasing measure.

* * *

"No eye has seen . . . what God has prepared for those who love him."
"Wait on the Lord . . . and he shall strengthen thine heart."
— 1 Corinthians 2:9, LB; Psalm 27:14, KJV

For Thought and Discussion

1. Where should the family altar be? What happens there?
2. What is the difference between TM and CM?
3. Read again the list of benefits derived from meditation and check the ones you'd like to have.
4. Memorize the Jesus prayer. Why is the name of Jesus so powerful?
5. Review the purpose of this book.
6. Practice for about five minutes (more when you wish) the simple ideas given on Christian meditation using the Jesus prayer.

5 *Being a Member of the Family*

In this chapter we will make a comparison study between God's family and a human family and what it means to be a member of each.

All of us are members of human families, even though some of them are badly divided and do not exhibit a real family relationship. And in one sense we are all one great big family in this world — the family of God. Every person who lives on this earth is a child of God by creation, for the breath of His life is in our nostrils. By physical birth, then, we receive these two gifts: the breath of life from God and relationship in a human family.

There is also a spiritual birth, a second birth, at which time the Holy Spirit of God is breathed into us (John 1:13; 3:5). This Spirit helps control the "bent to evil" and the sinful, selfish nature which plagues us all. Jesus Christ came to give us this second birth and to bring us back to the original purpose for our creation, which is *that God might enjoy us.* This spiritual birth gives us the greatest gift of all: membership in God's family.

Did you ever stop and say to yourself: "God made me

so that He could enjoy me"? Well, stop now and say it, for it is true. To be sure, most of us have forgotten this and have become hell-bent on enjoying ourselves regardless.

Five Questions

Question #1: Does your family enjoy you? Do you enjoy your family? How does one enjoy another person?

Answer: By being with them, getting to know them, talking together, doing things together, sharing thoughts and things. Understanding, love, and caring with deep appreciation will soon follow.

To Think About: Where do you "miss the mark" with your own family? How do you score on "enjoying God" or letting Him enjoy you? Loving God means all those things, too. Read the above answer over again thoughtfully.

Question #2: Since a family is related, please define this relationship.

Answer: There are three legal ways one becomes related. *By marriage,* two people become related as husband and wife. *By birth,* a child becomes related to his parents. *By adoption,* a child becomes related to his parents. (Adoption and birth also include being related to other blood relatives.)

Question #3: In what way are we related to God then?

Answer: Obviously, marriage is out. The other two, birth and adoption, are mentioned in the Bible as the means of becoming children of God (Rom. 8:15; Gal. 4:5; John 1:12,13). We are born into

God's family by faith when we call on the name of Jesus (this is prayer). We become His children by being born of His Spirit, who comes into us, making us new persons inside. The words *adoption* and *sonship* are used synonymously in many of today's versions of the New Testament.

Question #4: How does one come into this Father/son relationship with God?

Answer: Well, it *is* somewhat like marriage. There is something for both parties to do. In a human relationship, you admit and surrender to the fact that you two want to be one, that you want to spend the rest of your lives together. And you trust and believe one another. That's *your* part in the Father/son relationship — to believe what God says about His desire to have this relationship with you.

God's part has already been done. It was completed through the life, death, and resurrection of Jesus Christ, which makes new children out of us (2 Cor. 5:17; 1 John 2:12; 3:1). This new relationship is also God's gift to us. We receive it by believing on the person of Jesus Christ.

Question #5: Does it make any difference to whom we pray?

Answer: There is no right or wrong way to address God; all prayer that comes from the heart is heard, for we do not manipulate God with words. Simplicity helps, as do honesty and directness. However, right here we need a short lesson on the Trinity, for it is a mystery. A mystery is something we know but can't explain.

A Lesson on the Trinity

God is three Persons: God the Father; God the Son; and God the Holy Spirit.

Here are two illustrations which show how one thing can take three forms and yet still be one.

First: You are a father, but you are also a son and a brother. You are one person with three relationships which never become confused. *Second:* The formula for water is H_2O. It is a solid (ice), a liquid (water), and a gas (air). Again, one substance but three forms.

Please do not stumble over the names of God, for there are more than 300 in the Bible. Your heart and your Bible will teach you which to use. Sometimes you will want to say *Our Father.* At other times, *Dear Jesus* or *Lord Jesus* will bring Him very near to you. They are one, and the Father is pleased when His Son is thus honored (John 5:22,23).

Becoming Like a Child

1. Become like a little child in your heart. If you will remember that, prayer will be easier. Everything gets simpler before it gets profound. Jesus told us to become like children or we could never enter His kingdom. Once you make up your mind to let Him help you, it isn't difficult.

2. Pray like a child and say,

   Dear Jesus, I love You. I want to love You as I ought. Forgive me for all my sins against You and against other people.

3. This is a good time to start saying the *Jesus prayer.*
   Lord Jesus Christ, Son of God,
   have mercy on me, a sinner.
4. Or, affirm your faith like this:
   Lord Jesus, I believe You are the Son of God. I believe You died for my sins and rose again. I believe You do wash my heart clean from all sin and wrongdoing right now, and I am Yours forever.

5. Now is the time to give thanks. Use these and other short phrases which come to mind.

Thank You, dear Lord, for . . .
the gift of becoming a son
the forgiveness of my sins
making me a member of Your family
a thankful heart
a clean heart
helping me receive Your love
helping me forgive others
most of all, for Yourself, and
Your love to me.

Once you have gone through this heart exercise, you will have an inner assurance that you are a child of God — no more doubts. Then you can also bring your children into the family of God, one by one, when the time is right and they are ready. Children readily and easily come into God's kingdom.

Don't make the mistake of thinking that your child is too young to make such a decision. The other day a friend told me this story.

An invitational hymn was being sung in church, and a small girl standing near her mother said, "Momma, I want to go up. I want'a accept Jesus as my Savior."

"Be quiet. You're too young," her mother admonished her.

Again the child pulled on her mother's dress and made the same request. She got the same answer. Once more the child pulled on her mother and announced, "Mother, I just did it right here, Jesus already came into my heart."

Here are two stories about parents who helped their children pray and enter the kingdom.

The story of a mother and son

This mother had been attending my morning sessions on how to pray and how to help her children learn to pray. She stood waiting to speak to me after my talk.

"My son is fifteen years old, and already he is a junior deacon in our church. But in our family we never talk much on important subjects. In my own heart I am troubled because I don't think Tom has really given his heart to Jesus. What should I do?"

"Why not pray for an opportunity, and just ask him?" I suggested.

Her face brightened, and she thought she could do that. So for a moment, standing there, we "agreed in prayer" that such an opportunity might present itself.

The next morning she was late, and I had already started my teaching session when she entered, but one look at her face told me she had something to share with us.

"Last night, Tom was quite late coming in; all of us were in bed. But as he came up the stairs, I got up and waited to welcome him, saying, 'Tom, I have something to ask you, which only you can answer.' He waited, and I went on, 'In my heart I want to know for sure . . . have you ever accepted Jesus as your own personal Savior?'

"He said, 'No, but I've wanted to.'

"I said, 'Why not do it right now?' "

So they knelt beside Tom's bed and prayed together. Two of the smaller children had awakened and came in to kneel beside them also, and there was joy and rejoicing when the prayer was over.

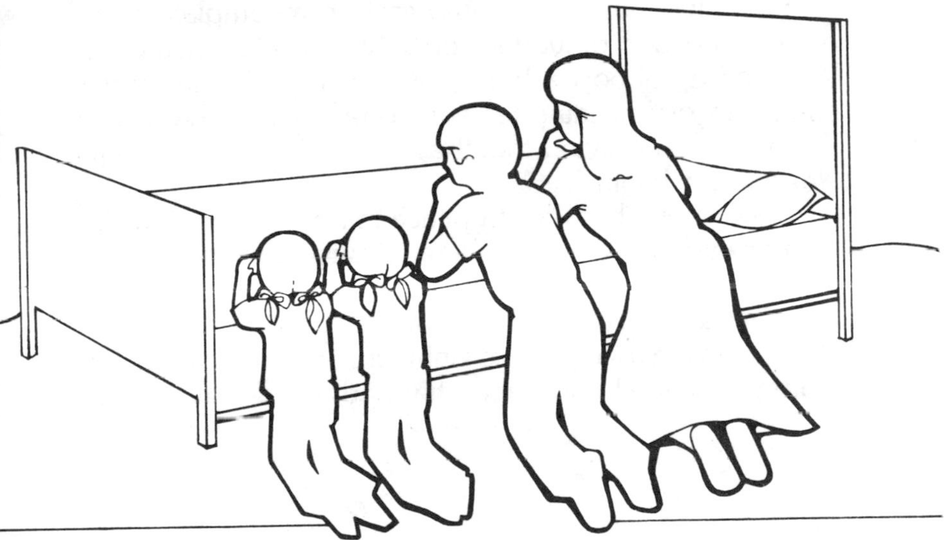

The story of a mother and her four children

Discouraged, depressed, and debating whether or not to start divorce proceedings, Lou was grateful for the friends who persuaded her to get away from it all for a week and go with them to the *Camp Farthest Out* held on an Ohio college campus.

One day after hearing me speak on conversational prayer, one of them asked, "Why don't we try this together here in our room?"

"I've never prayed aloud in my life," said Lou.

"Neither have I," protested the other friend.

However, the three pulled their chairs together, took hands, and started with the simple words they had just been taught: "I love You, thank You, please help me," etc.

Several months after that, when I was a guest in her home, Lou told me the rest of her story.

"We just poured out our hearts, our complaints, and our troubles and prayed for ourselves and for each other. We used up almost a box of Kleenex, and when it was over, with joy and laughter, someone looked at her watch. We had been praying together for two and a half hours! Not bad for beginners!"

Lou drove home with peace in her heart plus a new relationship between herself and Jesus, knowing she was not alone in the problem she faced.

As she drove into the driveway at home, her oldest child, Diane, a lovely girl of eighteen, ran out crying, "Oh, mamma, wait till you hear what daddy's done!"

Quietly her mother answered, "God is going to take care of him."

Diane's tears dried in quick surprise. "What's happened to *you?*"

Lou told her to come inside and she would explain. They went upstairs to Diane's room, where they were joined by the other three children, and there Lou told them what had taken place and how she had become a new child of God. She explained that because Jesus was in her and with her, she was going to trust Him for everything, including daddy and everybody else too. Right there, Lou led her children to Jesus, and on their knees together they all just talked to Jesus from their hearts, and He filled them with His joy and a tremendous love for each other.

Since then, I've been in their home a number of times and have watched the growth of love and maturity in that family.

God knows just the right time for your children to take this step of "declaring Jesus as their Savior" or "inviting Jesus into their hearts." Wait for that right time. Pray about it. Be aware and be ready. Their hearts are open, tender, and receptive.

For Thought and Discussion

1. What two gifts does God give us in physical birth?
2. What gift is given to us in spiritual birth?
3. Compare the two families — God's family and the human family — by using questions 1, 2, 3, 4. By using these words: enjoyment, relationship, birth/adoption.
4. Why is an understanding of the Trinity helpful in praying from our hearts?
5. Have you asked your child that important question? Question 4 and answer will help you.
6. Turn to *Becoming like a child* and, with eyes wide open, spend five quiet minutes as you think and talk to God about #2, #3, #4, and #5.

6 *Questions People Ask Me*

1. *What does a man do when his wife is unwilling to pray aloud with the family?*
2. *Can we start prayers with a three-year-old? Is that too young?*
3. *There just isn't time for the whole family to pray together every day. What can we do?*
4. *Should family prayers be before or after meals?*
5. *What about guests or visitors in the home when it is time for family prayers or saying grace the way you suggest? Should we change? Or skip it?*
6. *Did you ever run into a situation where a child refused to pray?*
7. *What should we read at family prayers? Just the Bible, or other devotionals or storybooks?*
8. *What kind of Bible should we use?*
9. *How should we read? Where do we start? Should the father always do the reading?*

10. *Is it all right to have short prayers most days of the week and one longer time once a week?*

11. *What do we do about the failures, sins, and inadequacies which plague us as partners and make us feel like hypocrites?*

Answers to Questions

Question #1: What does a man do when his wife is unwilling to pray aloud with the family? "She is a member of God's family, but because she came from a broken home, she never learned to pray with anyone else." Should he start alone and expect her to join when she wants to?

Answer: They should talk it over together. They talk about everything else: money, food, sex, the car, the neighbors, the children. Why can't they talk about God and prayer? Especially when they are considering goals and needs for the family.

Not wanting to pray aloud is an emotional block largely based on one's pride — fear of not being able to do it the right way. There is no right way to pray except one: pray from your heart as a little child.

Praying aloud does make you vulnerable. You will say things in prayer you would never say otherwise, because you are talking to God who loves you and understands you. If you will expose your real self, as you pray in your wife's presence, and ask God to help you with some weakness (which she already knows you have), she will probably speak right up and comfort you and love you — by praying for you! When weakness is revealed in the atmosphere of humble prayer, the result is always the same: those who listen will love you for yourself alone, and they, too, will find their defenses breaking down.

Take the risk! Try it and see for yourself.

Question #2: Can we start prayers with a three-year-old? Is that too young?

Answer: I have two stories for you on this subject.

The first is from Lorraine Murphy of California, who says, "I can't stress enough the value of teaching children to pray. Not just the prayers of the church, beautiful and valuable as they are, but the prayers that are 'just between You and me, God.' There's an old hymn that says, 'Take it to the Lord in prayer,' and that's what children should be taught. Otherwise, if they only take it to mommy and daddy, the parents will eventually become false gods. Taking it to the Lord *with* mommy and daddy is great to begin with, but then the transference of being able to take it to the Lord alone is the path to spiritual maturity.

"We have a granddaughter, Elizabeth, and I have started to teach her to pray. She's just delighted when I take her little hand and teach her to bless herself before eating. And when it comes to the 'Amen,' she folds those darling little hands and beams, because even at sixteen months she knows this is something very special and meaningful. Children imitate and absorb everything around them — why not a prayer life?

"Another area I can't omit is the wonderful opportunity of teaching children in junior choirs to pray. If they aren't being exposed to prayer at home, they can learn it at choir and take it home to share with the rest of the family. We are teaching them compassion and how to share, and how to receive from God, the giver of all good gifts."

The next story is about a three-year-old who taught his father to pray. Several years ago United Church Women in Emporia, Kansas, invited me for a city-wide prayer conference. They did a great job of organization and of drawing people in; I remember it as one of the most joyous conferences I ever conducted.

One of the women on the committee introduced me to her husband after the final dinner, explaining, "We are Roman Catholic, and this casual kind of conversing with God is new to us, but it has drawn our family together. My husband and I have learned to pray together."

I shook his hand, and he was a bit embarrassed, so I asked, "How did that happen?"

"After you taught the gals on the committee to pray this kind of talking-together-prayer with Jesus there, I went home thinking how nice it would be if we could do it together. I was a bit hesitant about approaching my husband — but there was my three-year-old son, Mikey. Why not teach him? But how? I even prayed about that, and then the idea hit me; I taught him, and we had lots of fun praying together.

"Then one night, with some apprehension, I overheard my little son say, 'Daddy, mommy taught me a game, and we're going to teach you, too. It's just like playing ball: I throw it to you, and you throw it back to me. Only we don't have a ball, we throw *words* . . . sit down . . . I'll show you.'

"He pulled his chair up, called for me to come, and

told us all to take hands, because *'Jesus is right here.'* Mikey prayed, 'Thank You, dear God, for my daddy. Now you throw it back to me, and say my name.'

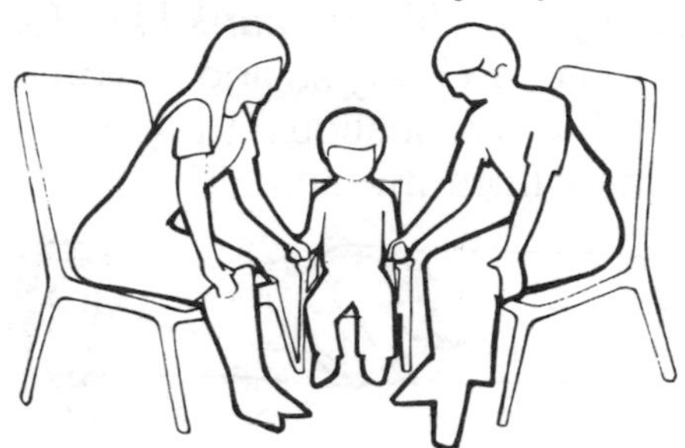

"Father, a bit awkwardly, 'Thank You, dear God, for Mikey.'

"Mikey, 'Thank You, dear God, for mommy.'

"Mommy, 'And thank You, dear God, for our Mikey.'

"Mikey, 'Now, mommy, you say it to daddy, and he'll say it back to you!' "

Such simplicity, love, and excitement were irresistible, and it worked. Soon they were thanking God for other people and other things. It became the highlight of each following day.

I assured the young husband that he had taken the greatest step possible to assure that Mikey would one day be a confident, dependable child with faith in God, for children begin to equate what God is like with both father and mother.

"It wasn't easy," he assured me, "but it works, and I'm glad we got started."

Question #3: There just isn't time for the whole family to pray together every day. What can we do?

Answer: You eat together every day, don't you? And find time for that? How about prayer before you eat? And I don't mean just a memorized grace, although there are times when that will do as a stopgap!

I mean, *use that time usually given to table grace to welcome Jesus to your table, to thank Him for each other and the food,* with everybody saying a word of thanks of some kind, even if it is repetitious. Prayer is never repetition when it comes from the heart.

Exercise in visualization

Close your eyes right now. Can you see your family around the table — waiting for grace? See and hear yourself (the father) saying, "Thank You, Lord Jesus, for Your love. Welcome to our table." Now hear the other members, one by one, also thank Him for something — until someone says, "And thank You for the food. Amen." That's it. But the meaning *you* put into it will make the difference. And Jesus present by invitation and by name will make the difference.

Question #4: Should family prayers be before or after meals?

Answer: Before meals, when you make them short, because food is ready. You can use thanks (step 1) and praise (step 2) so that everyone has a chance to speak (to share), which is important in building family unity.

After meals is the best time for family prayers, if you want an adequate time together. Before meals, the grace can be done in one or two minutes, even with everyone giving thanks, and is a kind of remembrance that Jesus Christ is the head of your home; it will also promote the habit of giving thanks instead of griping about things. After an evening meal, at least once a week, the family should clear the table, get their Bibles, and plan to spend at least ten minutes, gradually adding time as needed.

Illustration

While conducting a prayer workshop in Tucson, Arizona, I was the guest in a home where there were two teen-age boys. Their parents practiced conversational prayer, having been in my classes in Taiwan on my visit there in 1969. But I was surprised to find them doing all four steps while their hot meal was waiting on the table. I stole a glance at the boys and noticed they took part without enthusiasm and as briefly as possible.

Later, as their mother cleared the dining room and took care of the kitchen, I slipped into the living room where the boys were. I asked if they liked those long prayers before they ate. Wouldn't they like it better *after* they ate? They both lifted their heads and flashed eager smiles at me, "Do you think you could manage it?" Of course I could and did. The parents had never once thought of the effect upon the boys.

In finding the right time for your family, be sure you think about the children and what effect it will have on them. There is a right time and a wrong time for each family.

Question #5: What about guests or visitors in the home when it is time for family prayers or saying grace the way you suggest? Should we change? Or skip it?

Answer: I was often a visitor in Herb and Olive Butt's home when their large family was growing up, and my own life was enriched as I saw them reading the Bible and praying together. Your visitors will be enriched also, for the simplicity, honesty, and naturalness of God-with-us is needed by them too.

Never abstain because of guests. Just invite them as they sit at table, by saying, "We are glad you can join us in this simple way to give thanks." Brief your children earlier on being themselves and on giving thanks for their guests.

Question #6: Did you ever run into a situation where a child refused to pray?

Answer: I am thinking of a family where the parents, though good church members, only found Christ as a life-changing Savior about two years ago. When they started family prayers, the teen-agers held back silently. However, the honesty and vulnerability of both parents in praying for help with their own known faults won the children, and it wasn't long before they, too, were offering honest prayer for themselves.

Then there was a little girl who wouldn't pray because she'd had a fight with her sister.

I was teaching a family session in Europe, and at the close the families moved into small circles. I saw a mother and her two little girls just sitting, silently, not talking or praying. I went over, and the mother, who was holding the six-year-old, said, "Carol is not on speaking terms with her sister right now." I put my arm around Carol and said, "God loves you both, and your mommie loves you, too. Wouldn't you like to say, 'I'm sorry,' to your sister?" That was all that was needed. They put their arms around each other — all three of them — and started to pray together.

Then there was Pam. Pam was the younger daughter of a Presbyterian minister, and her mother was concerned that even at twelve years of age she refused to remain in the room when her parents were having family prayers.

Then the mother heard me teach a prayer workshop in Harrisburg, PA, and went home full of fresh hope for Pam. As soon as Pam came home from school, she went right to her room. Mother knocked at the door, was invited in, and sat down quietly and told Pam about the way I taught them to pray — like a child, simply, honestly, briefly; saying "I" when they meant themselves and not hiding behind the editorial "we"; only using "we" when they really meant everybody present.

At first Pam did not want to listen, but as her mother went on, she lifted her head and a new light came into her eyes.

"If you and daddy would pray like that, I'd stay," she said. "I can't stand the dry old dead things you keep saying over and over. I don't think God is like that."

The first night I spoke in that church, Pam brought a whole row of her friends to hear me speak on prayer.

* * *

Jesus said, "Let the children come to me. . . . then he took the children in his arms" one by one (Mark 10:14,16 LB).

Question #7: What should we read at family prayers? Just the Bible, or other devotionals or storybooks?

Answer: The Bible, first and always, with a copy for each member who can read. Storybooks and devotionals are good too, and you can use them in the evenings or as an alternative, but please — not all the time. Let the Bible be in your hands and in the hands of your children; read from it, mark it, and love it.

I have a special section of recommended books and materials listed at the back of this book that will assist you in choosing these supplementary materials. For devotional books I especially recommend the Graded Daily Bible Reading Material from Scripture Union and *God Is Great, God Is Good* by Rolf E. Aaseng (see back of book for details on these).

Question #8: What kind of Bible should we use?

Answer: Today there is such a wide variety of Bibles offered that it would be well worth your time to visit a good Christian bookstore and examine them for yourself.

When the members of your family are old enough to read, it is often interesting to have different versions or translations in order to compare and discuss the many slight variations of meaning — all of them enriching the reader.

I only want to mention two of them here, for it would take too long to list them all. Personally, I use the American Bible Society's *Good News for Modern Man* because of the size, the print, the paragraphs, and the illustrations.

For young people and children, I recommend Ken Taylor's free translation known as the *Living Bible.* It is published in many sizes and for all ages. *The Children's Living Bible* (same text) is the one you will want for your children. Let me tell you the story of the origin of this paraphrase, which will make it more meaningful to you.

Every morning Ken Taylor used to read some portion

of the Bible to his large family and then asked, "What did those verses tell us?" One morning he read the first chapter of Ephesians and was met by silence when he asked the question. He read it again. More silence and uneasy shifting about.

That morning while commuting to Chicago where he worked, he took out his small New Testament and a piece of paper and began to write the meaning of Ephesians, chapter one, in everyday language. The next morning he read it to his children, and at once he got some answers.

So each morning on that commuter train, Ken did more free translating of difficult passages, starting with the epistles of Paul, and then read them to the children during family prayers. As time went by, he put the whole Bible into plain, everyday English.

We call this *a paraphrased edition,* not a translation from the original language. Direct translations by scholars are called *versions* and are, of course, more accurate for the purpose of study.

A new *translation,* which is very readable and understandable, is the *New International Version,* published by Zondervan. This comes in a children's edition which has many aids for young readers, such as full-color maps and illustrations, articles on the Bible, Bible times and customs, and the individual books of the Bible, Memory Margin™, and a dictionary. All of these features were written especially for this edition for children.

Question #9: How should we read? Where do we start? Should the father always do the reading?

Answer: To begin with, I would suggest that you use the "30 Days of Daily Devotions" which I have prepared for Part III of this book. You will find adequate helps there to get you started. Part II will help you begin a short and simple prayer time with your family, right around your table.

By the time you finish these readings, you can start on one of the Gospels and read right through it, knowing what to look for.

Regarding reading: you may read the entire portion, as a parent; or you may call on one of the children to read; or you may take turns, verse by verse; or you may take turns according to age.

* * *

"Train up a child in the way he should go; and when he is old, he will not depart from it" (Prov. 22:6 KJV). He may depart for a time, but sooner or later, in time of great need when all else fails, he will know where to turn. Give your child this important heritage.

Question #10: Is it all right to have short prayers most days of the week and one longer time once a week?

Answer: Our grandfathers would turn over in their graves! But today's world is a hectic, frantic, busy world, and time runs out. When every member of the family has a different breakfast time, or none at all, then what? Saturday morning somebody gets up early and goes to work, or somebody sleeps in. Sunday everybody gets up and goes to church and Sunday school. (Or do they?) Families I know who have teen-agers find that if they set aside one night a week, after supper, for about fifteen or twenty minutes, that is about all they can manage.

Talk it over. Agree upon one night a week and plan for it, like any other engagement. When the schedule needs to be altered, do it gracefully. I predict that your children will look forward to this planned time of communication and being together. You might even want to have family prayers more than once a week!

Mormons set aside two hours every week for family devotions and prayers. Consequently, their youth receive religious training at home and family ties are strengthened. The dividends are enormous. Their example is something we all would do well to follow.

Question #11: What do we do about the failures, sins, and inadequacies which plague us as parents and make us feel like hypocrites?

Answer: You have run head-on into the difficulty of "if I sin, can I still be a child of God?" In other words, the problem of keeping the relationship when the fellowship is broken. I want to answer this with three points:

1. Confession restores seemingly broken fellowship, and let's make it "instant confession," shall we? Broken fellowship never breaks the relationship, any more than your son ceases to be yours because he gets arrested for smoking pot. (See 1 John 1, 2, 3, especially verses 1:1-10; 2:1,2; 3:6-8.) Read these passages in the King James or some other version, and then for comparison, read them in the *Good News for Modern Man,* which allows for the Greek verb on sin to mean "continuously sinning action."

And may the Holy Spirit give you understanding.

2. I refer you to my autobiography, *Within The Circle,* in which I tell how I had to relearn many things about being a Christian, having been taught that if I sinned I was a sinner and had to be "born into God's family" all over again. I found that teaching to be misleading, for once a child, always a child. The basis of this is to be found in the full meaning of Christ's death and resurrection.

3. So, you've failed to keep the Ten Commandments? The Ten Commandments were given as a guide, and no person can keep them except Jesus Christ, the Son of God. He reworded them in Mark 12:29-31. When someone asked Him which was the most important of the ten, Jesus replied,

"The most important one is this:
Hear, O Israel,
The Lord our God, the Lord is one;
Love the Lord your God
with all your heart,
with all your soul,
with all your mind
and with all your strength.
The second is this:
Love your neighbor as yourself"
(Mark 12:29-31 NIV).

Then Jesus upgraded that command to an impossibility. He taught: *This is My commandment, that you love one another as I have loved you* (John 15:12).

All your inadequacies and failures involve your fellow-man, and back of it all there is the root cause: Inability to love one another. Now we have hit the bull's-eye! The first duty of a believer is to love his brother. The only way that can be done (and I've tried them all) is to release and surrender the inner self, all of yourself, to Jesus Christ so His Spirit can live in you, work in you, motivate you.

This is a miracle and a great mystery, but then miracles happen when we become humble like children and are willing for God to teach us His ways, which are not like our ways. Our God is greater than you think He is.

I should add, for I am coming to believe it more and more the longer I live, that it is the Holy Spirit within who heals all the hurt places and the old memories and makes the new fruit of love grow in profusion.

For Thought and Discussion

1. Check the questions which help you the most and underline especially meaningful parts.
2. If you are in a class or group, decide together on the best way to get people involved in sharing their needs on these subjects so they can find release as they pray for one another.

Part II
For Parents and Children

7 *The Presence of God*

In the next four chapters, teaching is given on how to present the four basic parts of prayer (the four steps) to children. I have tried to simplify the language so that those children who can read will be able to read it for themselves and grasp it quickly.

If your children are pre-school, or just learning to read, you may find it necessary to enlarge on the meaning by adding words of explanation wherever you feel they should be included.

Step 1 — Jesus Is Here

In this lesson we are learning about the nearness of God and how very much He loves each one of us. When we say "Jesus is here," we are quoting from Jesus' own words in Matthew 18:20:

> "For where two or three gather together because they are mine, I will be right there among them" (LB).

Jesus and our Father are one. Just as your father is a husband and a father at the same time, but is still only one person. If you want to read what Jesus said about this, turn to John 14:8,9 (you could also read 14:1-7).

How do we get started?

We create an atmosphere of love. *First,* let's take hands and make a circle of love, right at the table, because *Jesus is here!* We believe it, and we say it out loud. Then we say grace.

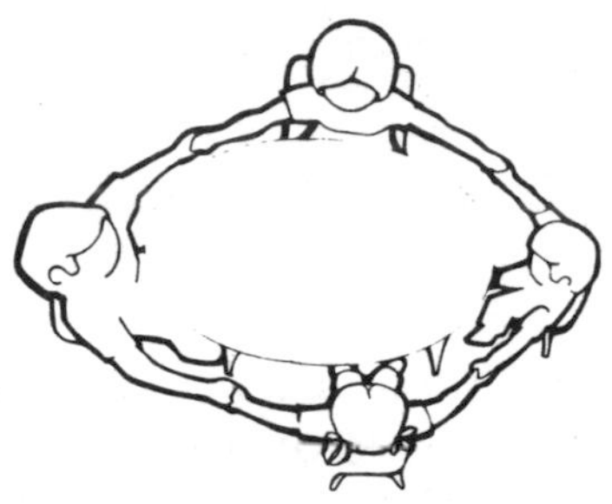

Or, for variety, change or add to the words above:

"Thank You, Jesus, for being here."

"God loves you, and I love you." (Say this to those sitting on each side of you, or parents say it to children.)

Making Jesus real

To make Jesus real to you, because He is there all the time, say His name. When I meet you, I say your name, because I'm glad to see you. Let's be glad when we say His name, too. When we say His name, we are welcoming Him.

We never talk to people who aren't there, do we?

The name of Jesus is full of power, full of love. He is always with us; He is always near us.

All day long, let us remember to call on His name when we are alone, or frightened, or hurt, or need help of any kind.

Let's start to talk to Him about everything. Some people talk to themselves. Do you? I've learned to talk to Jesus instead of talking to myself, because He knows everything, and He can do everything.

When you are afraid, say,
Jesus is here.
Thank You, Jesus.
You'll take care of me.

When you hurt yourself, say,
Jesus is right here.
Help me not to cry too much,
and make my finger well.

When someone else hurts you, say,
Jesus is here.
Jesus, You make it okay.
Thank You, Jesus.

When someone else gets hurt,
Put your hand out, touch him,
and say, *Thank You, Jesus,*
You can make him well.

The Four Steps

Here are all four steps of prayer in just four short sentences.

1. *Jesus is here* — the first step.
2. *Thank You, Jesus* — you are already saying the second step.
3. *Help me, Jesus* (or *Forgive me, Jesus*) is the third step, which means *I'm sorry* and is just as important as saying, *I love you.*
4. *Help my brother* is the fourth step. First we pray for ourselves and each other, and then for our friends who are not with us.

These four steps do overlap and get mixed up together when we pray, but that's the way it should be.

Testing

Can you say those four steps of prayer without looking at the page? Try it. Review them and say them to each other. Memorize them, because we are going to use them every day.

The Four Steps of Conversational Prayer

We Begin With His Presence

1. Jesus Is Here .... Matt. 18:19,20
Visualize Him. Use creative imagination and the Meditation card.
Be silent. Be a little child at His feet. He loves you.

2. Thank You, Lord .... Phil. 4:4-7
Gratitude is worship which opens the heart.
Be audible, brief, specific.
Use open-end prayer, don't close it.

We Pray for Persons Present and Absent

Thus Receiving and Giving Love

3. Forgive me, Lord .... James 5:13-16
Confession is a part of worship. Be honest.
Pray for yourself, then others will pray for you.
This is prayer response.
Say "I" when you mean yourself.
Say "we" when all present can be included.

4. Help my brother .... Mark 11:22-25
Prayer-response should be audible, brief with
love and thanksgiving. Use first names.
The Holy Spirit will give you words when you pray.
Give thanks when someone prays for you.
This is agreeing in prayer.

This Is Love In Action

Love one another as I have loved you................. John 15:12
Ask whatever you will and it shall be done............ John 15:7

This prayer from the heart is love in action. We become involved in God's purposes, in His view-point, and with each other's needs. Then the circle will widen to include family, friends, church, nation, the world.[1]

Meditation

1. My child, I love you.

I love you unconditionally.
I love you, good or bad, with no strings attached.
I love you like this because I know all about you.
I have known you ever since you were a child.
I know what I can do for you.
I know what I want to do for you.

2. My child, I accept you.

I accept you just as you are.
You don't need to change yourself.
I'll do the changing when you are ready.
I love you just as you are.
Believe this—for I assure you it is true.

3. My child, I care about you.

I care about every big or little thing which happens to you. Believe this.
I care enough to do something about it. Remember this.
I will help you when you need me. Ask me.
I love you.
I accept you.
I care about you.

4. My child, I forgive you.

I forgive you, and my forgiveness is complete.
Not like humans who forgive but cannot forget.
I love you. My arms are open with love.
Please come here! Come here to Me!
I forgive you.
Do not carry your guilt another moment.
I carried it all for you on the cross.
Believe this. It is true.

Rejoice . . . And Be Glad[2]

Teaching the love of Jesus

Read the Meditation slowly, with meaning, as if Jesus were saying it to your family through your lips. Ask them to close their eyes before you start. We can listen better with our eyes closed. The truth we hear sinks down into our subconscious minds to be used later. Don't be afraid of a little silence between sentences; it enables the words to sink in better. Keep in mind that you are realizing the presence and love of Jesus.

After the reading, with eyes still closed, ask each one to say a *Thank You, Jesus for . . .* (one of the four ways He loves you — more than one, if you like).

For Thought and Discussion

1. What four words (in the Meditation) tell us how much Jesus loves us?
2. What did we learn about *Jesus Is Here?*
3. Older children may wish to discuss the need for a family altar or for table grace. One of the children could lead the family prayers from time to time and think of many more things than I have suggested.
4. See the notes on this chapter at the back of the book for further available aids.

8 *The Miracle of Thankfulness*

Step 2 — Thank You, Lord

In this lesson we are teaching the prayer of thanksgiving, which in turn will help you acquire the habit of being grateful for everything.

Review

What four words in the meditation tell us how much Jesus loves us?

What did we learn about *Jesus Is Here?*

The value of giving thanks

Why should anyone say "thank you" to another?

Some people have a habit of complaining or finding fault with everything and everybody. The best way to cure that bad habit is to say, "I'm sorry, Jesus. Please forgive me." Then He will give you so much fresh joy that you can say, "Thank You, Jesus" for the gift of forgiveness and the gift of joy.

Why don't you start right now and begin to say "Thank You, Jesus" all the time, instead of griping. If you practice, you can form this good habit of giving thanks for everything — yes, everything. Why, you will even find yourself making excuses for people by saying, "Thank You, Jesus, he didn't really mean it." "Thank You, Jesus, it could have been worse." "Thank You, Jesus, You know how to handle him."

Assignment

For one whole day, give thanks for everything — even the bad things — just every single thing that happens. Report back to your family that evening. Be sure and tell them all that happened and what you said to Jesus.

Before we have more teaching on giving thanks, we should stop and ask some questions which everybody asks. (Let one person ask the questions, and the rest of the family can answer or discuss. The sentences in italics give some suggestions for your discussion.)

A. *About Jesus and God*

1. Have you ever seen a picture of God?
   Be sure there is a picture of Jesus in the room.
2. Where did you see it?
3. Where is Jesus now?
   Listen to their answers. The Apostles' Creed says He is sitting on the right hand of God.
4. Do you agree?
   Discuss.
5. Did Jesus tell us where He was going?
   Listen. Then, let's find it in the Bible (Matt. 28:20). He said more than that (Matt. 18:19,20).

6. How can Jesus be more than one place at one time?

   The Holy Spirit is the resurrected Jesus with us.

B. *About the Holy Spirit*

7. Who is the Holy Spirit?

   Same as above.

8. What name does Jesus give Himself?

   Helper. Read John 14:15-20.

9. Whom should we pray to? The Father, the Son, or the Holy Spirit?

   See chapter 5.

10. Who do you talk to when you pray? What do you call Him?

11. Since Jesus is always with us and lives in our hearts, is it okay to pray to Him?

    Yes, we can get closer to any person when we talk directly to him.

12. Can I pray to Jesus and to our Father in the same prayer?

    Certainly, for they are one.

13. Do people ever pray to the Holy Spirit?

    Yes, when they know something about Him.

Giving thanks makes us aware that Jesus is here

In this section there will be three creative exercises to help you use your imagination so you can both know and feel that our Lord Jesus is with you. They will be based on the Meditation we had in the last chapter (p. 74).

Sometimes it is hard to feel that Jesus is present. And it is true that we act our way into new ways of thinking; it is not true that we think our way into new ways of acting. What we put into words soon becomes very real to us. That is why we need to get into the habit of saying both *Jesus is here* and *Thank You, Lord.*

This also is true when it comes to other things like loving one another or forgiving one another. We need to say it in words.

Directions

Please — only do one of these exercises at a time, but you may do it as many times as you like. It gets better the more times you do it. Let one person read, slowly and with meaning, while praying inwardly that Jesus will help him.

1. First Exercise: *Jesus loves you* (John 15:9).

   "I love you, just as the Father loves me" (GN).

   a. Place a picture of Jesus on the table for all to see.
   b. Be quiet and look at Him for a moment and listen to these words (read first paragraph of the Meditation: "My child, I love you." Read it twice. Add any words that come to you.
   c. Allow another short silence to let it all sink into your hearts. Then have audible prayer. Speak up and thank Jesus in short sentences.

2. Second Exercise: *Jesus wants to hold you* (Mark 10:16).

   "Then he took the children into his arms and placed his hands on their heads and he blessed them" (LB).

   a. Close your eyes and think of Jesus sitting right there with you. Now He is going to get up and come and put His arms around you, each one of you, and tell you, "My child, I love you. I not only love you, I accept you just as you are."

Now read the second paragraph of the Meditation, which is about acceptance. After you have done this a few times, the Holy Spirit will put into your heart the words to explain more of the meaning. Do not be afraid to say them, for God blesses simple words of love and acceptance.

b. Be quiet and remember those words. Say the ones you remember over and over in your heart.
c. Now hold hands and have a "thank-You-Jesus-for-accepting-me" time to pray sentence prayers (all on this subject).

3. Third Exercise: *Jesus invites you to come* (Matt. 11:28-30).

> "Come to me and I will give you rest — all of you who work so hard beneath a heavy yoke. Wear my yoke — for it fits perfectly — and let me teach you; for I am gentle and humble, and you shall find rest for your souls; for I give you only light burdens" (LB).

a. Visualize Jesus standing here, holding out His hands. See the scars left by the nails in His hands, as He says to you, "Come to me, and I will give you rest. . . ." Read those verses again.
b. Also read the third and fourth paragraphs of the Meditation and then be quiet a moment, with closed eyes, to think about the words and the invitation of Jesus.
c. Now listen closely: I want you to let the flesh-and-blood you (your body) sit real still in your chair; but I want the real-you-in-your-heart to get right up and go into Jesus' arms or however you want to approach Him.
d. Close this time with a simple, "Thank You, Jesus,

for being here with us and loving us. Amen."

Afterwards: Ask the others if they would like to share what happened. One teen-ager said, "I got up and knelt at His feet and told Him how much I loved Him. I'll never forget those moments."

The importance of simplicity

This is a true story about the time I was a guest in Kansas at the home of Glenn and Sally Torrey.

We had just finished supper when Glenn said, "Ros, teach our family to pray together."

Looking at the two girls, aged about four and six, I reminded myself to keep it simple so they would be included.

"Well, first of all, we need a chair for Jesus, because He's here, and we're going to talk with Him."

The four-year-old said quickly, "I'll get a chair for Him." And she pulled her baby brother's highchair from over by the wall right up close to hers (the baby was asleep upstairs).

Suddenly she was troubled. "Will Jesus sit in a highchair?"

"Why don't you ask Him?"

She was silent for a moment as she looked toward the chair. Then she smiled happily. "Yes, He says He will."

So we started with the first step, *Jesus Is Here,* and each of us said, "Thank You" to Jesus and "I love you" to each other.

During the next step, *Help Me, Lord,* father prayed first: "Lord, will you assist me to give an adequate witness to my colleagues in the history department, that I may glorify Your name."

Silence.

Then I had courage to say, "Glenn, do you think you could make that a little simpler so the girls could pray for you?"

And he did. "Dear Jesus, please help me to talk to those guys I work with at the college about You."

The girls picked it right up, almost word for word, and prayed for their daddy. "Dear Jesus, please help daddy to tell the guys he works with about You." And we all agreed by simply saying, "Thank You, Lord, we know You will answer that prayer."

That was our family prayer time right there at the table after supper.

Do you think your family could do that?

I know they could if you ask Jesus to help.

* * *

> "Some people brought children to Jesus for him to touch them, but the disciples scolded those people. When Jesus noticed it, he was angry and said to his disciples:
>
> > 'Let the children come to me!
> > Do not stop them, because
> > the Kingdom of God belongs
> > to such as these.

> Remember this!
> Whoever does not receive the
> Kingdom of God like a child
> will never enter it.'

Then he took the children in his arms, placed his hands on each of them, and blessed them" (Mark 10:13-16 GN).

To remember

Parents, keep your praying and talking on your children's level.

Children, if your parents pray big words, love them anyway and remind them of what I said here.

For Thought and Discussion

1. For one whole day, give thanks for everything — even the bad things — just every single thing that happens. Report back to your family in the evening. Be sure and tell them all that happened and what you said to Jesus.
2. *Parents,* keep your praying and talking on your children's level.
3. *Children,* if your parents pray with big words, love them anyway and remind them of what I said above.

9 *The Healing of Confession*

Step 3 — Help Me, Lord
Forgive Me, Lord

Teaching

In this step we are learning about the healing power of forgiveness and the prayer of confession. Let's begin by learning some important words and definitions and what they mean.

Words and definitions

Confession: to admit in words our faults to God and to each other.

Forgiveness: to pardon, to forget and put away what hurt us; to stop feeling resentful or mad and love again.

Response: to hear what our brother prayed and answer his prayer by praying aloud for him and with him.

Absolution: God's forgiveness is given when we confess — when we confess or admit — and we need to say that to our brother in our "response" prayer. He needs to hear it said to him, too. "If we confess our sins to him, he can be depended on to forgive us and to cleanse us from every wrong" (1 John 1:9 LB).

Affirmation: an affirmation is something like "comforting," because by saying in our prayer that we still love a person, and believe in him, it gives comfort and assurance. Wait until it's your turn and someone does it for you. You'll see. We "affirm" each other by this kind of praying.

I'm sorry, it's my fault

Nobody, especially me, likes to say, "I'm sorry. It was my fault. Please forgive me." That is because there is pride in my heart and I like to be right. Don't you? But nobody is right all the time. Sometimes it is only 80 percent my fault and 20 percent the other person's fault, and then sometimes it is just the opposite.

It is very hard for parents to say "I'm sorry," because they are older and because they are parents. But when a father can say "I'm sorry" to his teen-age daughter, something wonderful happens, and they can really love one another.

When I was on one of our American bases in Italy, I had dinner with some of the families and afterwards spoke to them about having family prayers. Then I asked each family to make a small circle, hold hands, and say, "I'm sorry" and "I love you."

Suddenly a teen-age girl ran to me, crying, and put her arms around me. She didn't want to make a circle of love with her family, but I quietly urged her to go ahead. She was so upset that she couldn't walk; she actually slid along the floor to her family group. I saw them put their arms around each other as they prayed, and then there were tears and smiles and more hugs.

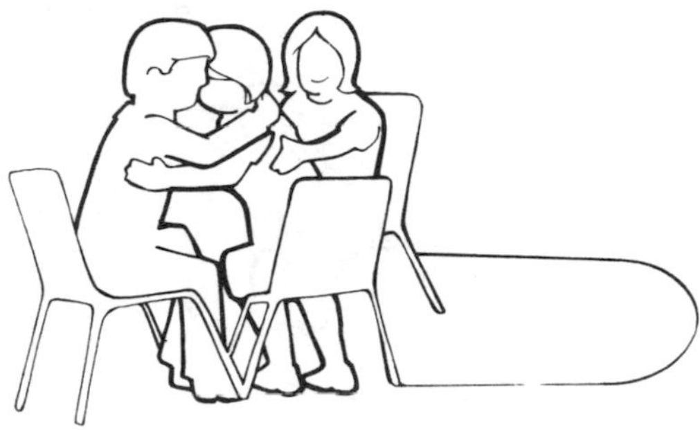

Her mother explained it to us afterwards. Her husband was the girl's stepfather, and they had never gotten along well because he was always reminding her of her diet, and she didn't seem to be able to lose any weight. So she became very resentful and avoided him all she could. That night they both asked each other's forgiveness, and God poured buckets of love all over that family! It was beautiful.

When we can ask God to forgive us and put it into words, it seems to be easier to ask our brother or sister, our mother or father, to forgive us. Then the miracle happens. Forgiveness is a gift from God, because He loves us and He wants us to love one another.

The story of two brothers

One night dad came home, and mother met him at the front door. "John, the two boys are in the living room waiting for you. It's one of those who-done-it-things, and I can't get a word out of either of them."

(Their father told me that it was none of my business *what* they had done, and I never did find out.)

Dad found the boys in the living room, both sitting on the sofa waiting for him — not speaking. So he sat down on the floor in front of them and looked up at them — I guess so he wouldn't be a big, terrible dad standing over them.

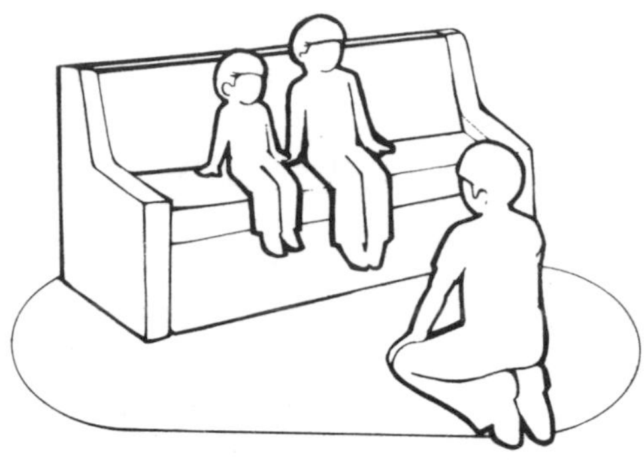

"Well, now, we want to find out who did it."

Silence.

Looking from one to the other, he said, "One of you boys did it. I know that, and you know it. The neighbor boys couldn't have done it, and I want an answer. Who did it? Which one of you?"

No answer.

"I'm not going to sit here all night waiting for you guys to come clean. One of you did it. Did you?" He pointed to the older son.

"Dad, do you think I'd do anything like that?" the older brother said reproachfully.

"Well, how about you?" pointing to the younger son.

"Honest, cross-my-heart-and-hope-to-die, I didn't do it," declared the younger one.

Dad looked first at one and then at the other and shook his head. "Something is wrong here for sure, and if you don't tell me, I'll have to — ." he stopped and waited.

Still no answer. More silence.

Finally dad had had it. "Okay, you two, if you don't tell me, I'm going to pick on one of you, give you a good spanking, and send you to bed."

And who do you think he picked on? The younger one. Don't ask me why. Maybe he was the one who got into trouble all the time anyway. I don't know. Anyway, he got a spanking and was sent to bed.

The next morning the boys came down for breakfast, and because this family was learning to pray together, father put out his hands as usual. "Jesus is here at our table." The rest of them took hands and answered, "Yes, Jesus is here."

Now for the next step — "Thank You, Lord."

Guess who prayed first? You're right. The younger brother.

"Dear Jesus, thank You . . . because you helped me to forgive my daddy for spanking me last night . . . when I didn't do it!"

When the father told me that part, I asked, "What did you do then?"

"I put my arms around that little fellow and asked him to forgive his daddy and that I was sorry; and we had a good hugging time."

About this time, mother was busy at the other end of the table. The older brother was in deep trouble. He'd lied to both parents and he'd let his little brother take his punishment.

With her arm around her oldest son, mother prayed

for him. And between his tears and his shame at being found out, he prayed, too, and asked Jesus to forgive him. He asked his brother to forgive him, and his mother and father too. And they all did!

Just think of the joy in that family that morning. There is no happiness like the happiness which comes when we get to the bottom of a lie and when Jesus makes us clean and forgives us. It is just as if it never happened. And the best part of it is, we love each other more than ever.

I know another story about two sisters who never did forgive each other for twenty years, and it made one of them sick. She asked me to pray for her, and God healed the sickness and also the deep resentment in her heart. Then she forgave her sister. I was there when it happened. It was beautiful!

What we can learn from these stories

That it pays to be honest,
To take off the goody-goody masks,
To say it like it is,
To respond to one another,
To forgive one another,
To affirm one another,
To pray for one another,
To be filled with joy and love,
To feel all clean inside again,
Because God forgives us
And our brother forgives us.

Getting off to a good start

Now that you've read these stories about families who got things fixed up God's way — by admitting and praying and forgiving — here are a few suggestions for getting started in your own family.

1. Start by being honest with each other when you pray. To be honest is important, because it removes a load of guilt from us and helps us listen to each other. If we can't listen to each other, how can we really love each other? It is hard sometimes to tell the truth, but hard things have a way of turning into good things.

2. Here are some things we say to other people but not to the persons themselves — because it is too hard.

My mother doesn't really know me at all.
My father doesn't understand me.
My husband doesn't want to listen to me.
My wife doesn't understand the pressures I'm under.

When we can open our hearts to each other and love is there, the truth comes tumbling out and all the dark places are exposed to the light. Then Jesus can heal us. Then we get to know each other. We can do this by listening to each other when we pray together.

3. Start today by saying *Jesus is here.* Then go right on to *Help me, Lord* or *Forgive me, Lord.* After supper, right at the table, is a good time and place to start.

4. Show others in your family that you care about things in their lives. One of them has an exam coming up, another a basketball game. Learn more about your children and what they are thinking. Likewise, children get to know your parents better. Praying together means you have time to listen.

5. Your family prayer-time might sound like this:

Bill: "Jesus, help me with that exam I've got tomorrow."

Father: "Thank You, Jesus. I know You will help him as he studies."
All: "Yes, thank You, Jesus."
Mother: "Thank You for helping our family to pray together."
Susy: "Forgive me, Jesus, for quarreling with Jimmy."
Jimmy: "Forgive me too, Susy. It was mostly my fault."
Mother: "Thank You, Jesus, that You forgave them both the moment they asked for forgiveness. Give us all love for one another and help us to act like it."
All: "Yes, Lord."
Father: "Please help Jimmy with that basketball game coming up tomorrow, and teach him to be a good loser as well as a good winner."
Jimmy: "Thank you, dad. And thank You, Jesus."

Everybody looks up and smiles, and you all say "Amen" at the same time. And mother says, "Praise the Lord!"[1]

The affirmation, response, and caring shown by what that family just said in their prayers tell the children that the parents not only care, but they listen. This means approval and acceptance, and those in turn mean strength and courage to do what God says we ought to do. When your family prays together, don't be in a hurry to stop, because someone else might want to pray.

For Thought and Discussion

1. Q. Is there any right or wrong way to pray?
   A. No, there isn't. There are many ways to pray.
2. Q. What does it mean to be childlike when we pray?
   A. To be open, honest, trusting, simple, and brief.

3. Q. Does Jesus love us when we are bad?

A. He loves you all the time, because He knew all about it before you ever did it. He loves you, but He does not like what you did.

4. "Amen" at the end of a prayer means "Good-by for now, Jesus." In the middle of a prayer it means "So be it," or "I agree."

5. Remember, there isn't one thing you can do to make God love you more, and there isn't one thing you can do to make Him love you less. The reason is: He is love, and He never changes. Not ever.

10 *Praying for Others*

Step 4: Help My Brother

In this step we will learn how to pray for one another. We will begin by discussing three kinds of people and how to pray for them.

1. *Those who are with us in person.* That is, usually the person with me who has just prayed for himself or who is too shy to pray aloud. He needs the *prayer of response and affirmation.* We affirm and comfort someone when we pray *with* him, especially when we have just listened to what he prayed. We make it a point to thank God for him. It only takes a sentence or two.

2. *Friends who are absent* —when we do not know what to ask for or what to pray for. Since all things are known to God, we pray the *prayer of love,* by saying, "Lord, surround Carol with your love today. All day long, behind her, in front of her, on both sides of her, above her and below her. Like a cloud . . . just surround her . . . and I send my love to her too."

3. *People we do not know at all,* but whom we care about. Like, earthquake or famine victims, families you read about in the newspapers who have tragic things happen, our government, our president, men and women in the armed forces, missionaries, and believers in other countries . . . and many more which you may think of at the time. This is called *the prayer of intercession,* which means asking God to intercede (to act) in mercy and favor toward the other person and to do whatever is best for him.[1]

We can pray all these prayers for anyone, but I have listed them in this order to make them easier to remember. The following Bible verses tell us more about these three kinds of prayer: Philippians 1:9-11,19; Luke 11:5-13; James 5:14-16.

How to pray

Some people think "conversational prayer" is saying sentence prayers. The trouble with that definition is that the sentence prayers are usually "unrelated sentence prayers."[2] We should all pray for *one subject* or *one person at a time,* until we can say "Thank You, Lord." Then another can pray or make a request by prayer. If you do it by "talking," it sometimes turns into gossip or gets pretty lengthy. Just tell Jesus what you know He can do and what your heart tells you to pray.

We should always pray for a person by name and with love. We should not be anxious, nor plead, nor worry. We should not tell God about the other person's sins. He knows already. We can make our requests with thanksgiving and praise, because Jesus loves all of us and wants to give us good things (Phil. 4:6-8; James 1:5).

Prayer for sick persons

The verses in James 5:14-16 tell us how to pray for someone who is sick. Ask other Christians to come and pray with you. When we add our faith together, that means more faith. We don't always need the oil; we can just put our hands on the sick person (his head or shoulders or wherever it hurts), for touching shows we care. Our hands have no healing, because Jesus is the Healer; but He works through us, by our love and prayers and hands if we ask Him and give Him the praise. It is not only our bodies that get sick; our feelings can be hurt, and He can heal them too. He can do anything. He does miracles for all who ask.

"Ask and you shall receive" is His promise to us.

The prayer of a five-year-old

Recently I was asked to be present at a women's meeting at Our Lady of Guadalupe, a Catholic church in Santa Ana, California. Father Daley had been using my books to teach the women to pray with their children, and some wonderful stories came out of that meeting.

One is about a five-year-old boy who prayed for his baby sister. His mother had taught the children to pray for *everything* and about everything that happened to them. The baby sister was three months old, and she had an eye infection; the prescribed drops weren't helping, and her little eyes were filled with mucus.

So the five-year-old said, "Let's all pray for her and put our hands on her. Jesus can heal her." So they did.

The next morning he ran to tell his mother that little sister's eyes were all well. Sure enough they were! Then he said, "Let's turn off the TV and say, 'Thank You, Jesus.' " And they did.

Two women hearing this story admitted that they had friends who were ill or in the hospital, but they were afraid to lay hands on them and pray, for fear nothing would happen. They thought it might discourage the patient. We taught them, then, that the power belongs to Jesus; we don't have any. We are only the "in-between-pipeline" to carry the power of Jesus. He is all powerful. He is the Healer. We pray in His powerful name.

Physical healing comes in many ways. Sometimes it comes slowly; sometimes it happens quickly. But always there is a healing of our spirits when our bodies are healed — our feelings and emotions are healed.

When you pray, right during the prayer try to picture the person as already healed and give thanks. This is important. Read Mark 11:24: "When you pray and ask for something, believe that you have received it, and everything will be given you" (GN).

For Thought and Discussion

1. Jesus is the Healer. Let's trust Him.
2. Why are some people not healed? (Perhaps it is not God's time for them to be healed.)

3. What is the Christian attitude toward death? (When people are very old, they often say, "I've finished my work on earth. I want to go home and be with Jesus. I'm praying He will come for me." And He does, for their work is ended and He wants them in heaven with Him. This is the attitude Christians should have toward death.)

Part III
30 Days of Daily Devotions

30 Days of Daily Devotions

Daily Procedure

1. *Grace at the table*

a. A memorized "grace" for each child can be used.

b. The first part of the daily outline can be used, and this will produce spontaneous and honest prayers. Saying "Jesus is here" or "Thank You, Lord" does not threaten anyone and gives all a chance to take part, which is important in developing family unity. Whoever wants to close the thank-you time can pray, "Thank You, Lord, for this food. Amen."

c. See chapter eight for more help on the thank-you's.

2. *The Bible reading and questions,* which are the second part of the daily outline, can be used every day, twice a week, or once a week, depending on what your family decides. Write the dates on the pages you have just finished to remind you, and mark the calendar, too. Ask the children to help you.

3. *The best place* for the family altar is right around the table after the meal, not before. One woman took her

children into the living room and wondered why nothing happened; they were too far apart and not accustomed to intimate conversation in that room.

4. *Encourage each child to have his own Bible.* Teach them to learn the books of the New Testament; make a game of finding references (verses). The first one who finds can read.

5. *Reminder for parents*

Let the children read . . . do not do all the reading.

Let the children talk . . . do not do all the talking.

Let the children pray . . . do not do all the praying.

If you fail in these three things and they do not respond, there are problems. They may be afraid or they may be sullen because they feel you are not fair or honest in other areas. They can withhold themselves from you by not praying. It is your responsibility to find out what's troubling them. Perhaps the child feels dominated. Have you given him a fair chance to tell his side of the story? Have you listened to him, without interrupting him or getting angry? Why not give it a try?

Daily Outline

To prepare you for the daily devotions.
To keep the subjects in mind.
To simplify the procedure.
To visualize the outline.

The Pattern

	(1. Jesus is here.	Use to begin with.
Morning (or meals)	(	Use for table grace.
	(2. Thank You, Lord.	Use at any time.
	(1. Bible Reading	Use at least once
You choose the time	(	a week.
	(2. Questions or Discussion	
	(1. Praying for myself	Use once a day
Evening (or any time)	(	at the table,
	(2. Praying for you	in the car,
	(	before bed,
	(3. Praying for others	anywhere!

Please study the pattern or outline above and notice that there are three main parts to each devotional. Memorize them. Stop and visualize them being done by your family. Repeat them to each other.

FIRST WEEK

Subject for the week: The Person of Jesus Christ

Who are You, Lord, that I might believe in You? — Acts 9:5-20; John 9:35-38

Comments: Who is this man, Jesus? We must know *in whom* we believe, a Person — not merely *what* we believe. Faith in Christ comes by (1) answering God's invitation (2) choosing to be His follower and (3) by reading the Bible; these three help to bring inner assurance so that you will know *who you are:* a beloved child of God!

1st day: What did John the Baptist say about Jesus?
2nd day: What does God the Father say about Jesus?
3rd day: What did the common people say about Jesus?
4th day: What did the "religious" Pharisees say about Jesus?
5th day: What did the disciples say about Jesus?
6th day: What did the apostle Paul say about Jesus?
7th day: What do you say about Jesus?

Read these daily titles aloud to your family and see what they already can tell you about each one. Do they know where to find them in the Bible?

Day 1: *What did John the Baptist say about Jesus?*

Morning (or meals):

Jesus is here. (Say it. You will soon believe it!) Thank You, Lord. (Thank Him for each other by name.)

Bible Reading:

a. Who is this John? Mark 1:1-6
b. What was his message? Mark 1:7,8
c. What was Jesus coming for? Mark 1:8; John 1:6-9,15,16

Questions:

a. Is it more important to know a person or to know about a person? Give an example.
b. Do you know anyone baptized with John's baptism?
c. Do you know anyone baptized with Jesus' baptism?

Evening (or any time):

My prayer:	Anyone can start and be the first person to pray. Ask for what you want.
Your prayer:	Anyone can respond or agree to that prayer. Then repeat the pattern: You ask, and I'll pray for you.
Our prayer:	After we've prayed for those present, we can pray for others not present.

To remember:

You do not need to say "Amen" or "for Jesus' sake" after every person's prayer — only when you are ready to close — because we are having a conversation with Jesus.

Day 2: *What does God the Father say about Jesus?*

Morning:

Jesus is here. (Each one say it and be glad.)
Thank You, Lord (for being here, etc.).

Bible Reading:

a. When Jesus was baptized. Mark 1:9-11
b. When Jesus was troubled. John 12:27-33
c. When Jesus knew the cross was coming. Mark 8:34

Questions:

a. Frank Laubach once said to me, "God is speaking all the time, all the time, all the time." What do you think He is saying to you now? Let's stop and listen as we get ready to pray.

Evening:

My prayer: Tell Jesus what you think He said to you.
Your prayer: Respond or answer the first one who prayed. Then pray yours, and he responds (like playing ball).
Our prayer: Send God's love to the people you think of now.

To remember:

Jesus is here, and He hears you. So make your prayers short, simple, and brief so everyone can have more than one turn if he wants it.

Day 3: *What did the common people say about Jesus?*

Morning:

Jesus is here. (Each one say it aloud.)
Thank You, Lord. (Each one thank Him for something.)

Bible Reading:

a. Luke 4:36; 5:26 They were ____________.
b. Mark 6:2 They were ____________ at him.
c. Mark 1:27 This man has ____________.
d. John 4:29 Could he be ____________?

Question:

If you had been there, what would you have said? ____________________

Evening:

My prayer:	I'm sorry, (Mom), please forgive me. And I'm sorry, Jesus, please forgive me.
Your prayer:	Lord, thank You that You forgive (Jim) right now, and I forgive him too (or something similar).
Our prayer:	For someone sick or in need, but not present.

To remember:

Jesus wants you to believe in Him and to tell Him so . . . many times a day. Tell Him also that you love Him.

Day 4: *What did the "religious" Pharisees say about Jesus?*

Review: The subjects of the past three days.

New: The *Pharisees* were a Jewish religious party; they were very strict in obeying the law of Moses and other regulations which had been added to it through the centuries.

Morning:

Jesus is here. (Say it with expectancy.)
Thank You, Lord. (Let it come from your heart.)

Bible Reading:

a. John 11:53. What was the Pharisees final plan?

____

b. John 11:1-44. What miracle happened just before this?

____

c. John 11:45-50. Why were they so upset and angry?

____

Personal question: Do you know any modern-day "Pharisees"? What do they say about Jesus?

Evening:

My prayer:	Ask forgiveness for being a judge and condemning others. Only God is the judge.
Your prayer:	For yourself, but for me if I prayed first; then I'll pray for you. "Thank You, Jesus, for helping him be honest."
Our prayer:	For all who judge and condemn others and do not love and pray for them.

To remember:

When you pray for yourself, you say "I" or "me"; when you include others, you say "we" and "us." This is honesty. God hears an honest prayer and forgives.

Day 5: *What did the disciples say about Jesus?*

Morning:

Jesus is here. (Read it from Matt. 18:19,20.) Thank You, Lord . . . for . . . . (You add whatever you think of.)

Bible Reading:

a. Luke 8:22-25. What danger were they in?

____

What question did Jesus ask?

____

What question did they ask?

____

b. Mark 8:27-29. What questions did Jesus ask?

____

What answers did He get?

____

Mark 8:30-33. Why were they not to tell?

____

(Answer: Because Jesus was sure about the future events, and they were not.)

Evening:

My prayer: Pick out a verse we've read and tell Jesus from that verse what you'd like to do and what you'd like to be.

Your prayer: Respond to mine first; then pray yours. I'll respond by praying for you, too. Let the whole family do this for each other.

Our prayer: For all the people we know who love Jesus — name as many as you can, and as you do, lay their names at Jesus' feet for Him to bless.

To remember:

We must pray for one another when we are together to encourage each other. This is a good way to show that we love one another.

Day 6: *What did the apostle Paul say about Jesus?*

New: Who is the apostle Paul?
A former persecutor of early Christians who became a great missionary and wrote many of the New Testament books. His teachings became a bridge between Jew and Gentile.

Morning:

Jesus is here. (Right here at our table.)
Thank You, Lord . . . for. . . . (Name daily blessings.)

Bible Reading:

a. Colossians 1:15-22. Name the things Paul believed about Jesus in this famous passage.
b. Philippians 2:1-11. Here is another great passage. As believers in Jesus, how should we look out for each other (verses 2-4)?

Evening:

My prayer:	With eyes open, looking at the passage in Philippians, tell Jesus what *you* believe about Him.
Your prayer:	Each one of you do the same thing.
Our prayer:	For friends (name them) who do not yet believe in Jesus.

To remember:

God had a plan for Paul's life, and He has a plan for each of us. We find it by keeping close to Him. He shows it to us a step at a time.

Day 7: *What do you say about Jesus?*

Review: What have you learned during these past six lessons?
Tell what you remember best.
Which Bible verse tells us who Jesus is?
Find it, underline it, write it on the flyleaf of your Bible so you can find it easily.

Morning:

Jesus is here. (Announce it gladly; welcome Him.)
Thank You, Lord. (Make being thankful a daily habit.)

Bible Reading:

a. John 1:1-16. This is one of my favorite passages, about the deity of Jesus Christ: that means, who He is. He and the Father are one.
b. John 5. A complete chapter on the oneness of the Father and Son.

Evening:

My prayer:	Forgive me, Lord, that I forget who You are; forgive me that I don't obey You as I ought.
Your prayer:	The same.
Our prayer:	Whatever is in your hearts, pray it aloud together.

To remember:

Each of us must kneel at the feet of Jesus and say, "My Lord and my God, I believe in You."
Find a place alone today and tell Him.
Read John 20:19-29.

SECOND WEEK

Subject for the week: What Jesus said about Himself.

Comments: In studying the identity of Jesus (who He is), we look at the *indirect claims:* what He did, all His miracles. We also look at *direct claims:* what He said.

1st day: I AM the Light of the World.
2nd day: I AM the Bread of Life.
3rd day: I AM the Good Shepherd.
4th day: I AM the Way, the Truth, and the Life.
5th day: I AM the Vine.
6th day: I AM the Resurrection and the Life.
7th day: I AM who I AM.
I AM He (the Messiah) walking with you.

Everything in this world battles for our minds. Let us pray for the gift of concentration while we study each one of these lessons.

To remember:

Our president doesn't go around claiming in so many words who he is! He just acts like he should as president of the United States. Jesus acts like He should as Creator of the universe.

Day 1: *I AM the Light of the World.*

To memorize: John 8:12. Turn to this verse, underline it, and then memorize it.

Morning: Jesus is here . . . we welcome You, Lord Jesus. Thank You, Lord . . . for being here with us. *Remember:* Everybody says both of these things.

Bible Reading:

Turn to the passages and let each read a few verses. John 1:1-12. John 12:44-50.

Questions:

a. How many things can you tell about light?
b. What do we do to become children of light?
c. How is Jesus the Light of the World?

Evening:

My prayer: Think of Jesus, the Light, when you make your prayer something like this: "Lord, shine into the dark corners of my heart and make them clean."

Your prayer: Agree with mine; then pray the same prayer for yourself.

Our prayer: For all who are teachers of God's light. For all who are receiving that light. For all who are still in the darkness of unbelief.

To remember:

Our prayer today was more general. We make it specific by saying a name, or an act, or a sin. Specific prayers get specific answers.

Day 2: *I Am the Bread of Life*

To Memorize: John 6:35. Underline it. Learn it now. Review yesterday's verse. Be sure and learn the reference along with the verse.

Morning: Jesus is here! (Each one of us tells the other!) Thank You, Lord. (Time for being thankful.)

Bible Reading:

Turn to John 6:25-51; some may use different translations.

Questions:

a. What "creation" miracle took place in the first part of this chapter?
b. Underline all these words in your Bible: believe, see, come, comes.
c. What do we eat bread for? Why is believing in Jesus like eating bread? Or coming to Jesus? Or seeing Jesus?
d. Name the two kinds of bread Jesus talks about.

Evening:

My prayer: "I'm sorry, forgive me for ____________ (be definite).

Your prayer: "Thank You, Jesus. You forgive him, and I do too." Then say your own prayer.

Our prayer: For our friends who need the Bread of Life or who are in need of any kind.

To remember:

When anyone asks forgiveness, we must give it quickly and *affirm* them. (Affirm means letting them know we love them by responding or answering or agreeing with them.)

Day 3: *I AM the Good Shepherd*

To memorize: John 10:11

Morning: Jesus is here! (Announce it to each other with joy!)
Thank You, Lord, for being here, and thank You for ____________. (Name those on each side of you.)

Bible Reading:

John 10:1-30

Questions:

a. Find the four things the Shepherd does (vv. 12,14,28,29).
b. Find the four things the sheep do (vv. 3,4,14,16).

Evening:

My prayer: "Forgive me, Lord, for . . ."
Your prayer: Respond or pray for him. Then it's your turn.
Our prayer: For others, by name, being sensitive to their needs and what God wants to do for them.

To remember:

Be short, be simple, be brief. But be sure to be personal and honest. That means being vulnerable; but it also means you will feel loved. (Vulnerable means: easy to get hurt.)

Day 4: *I AM the Way, the Truth, and the Light.*

To memorize: John 14:6. Review the other three now.

Morning: Jesus is here. ("For where two or three are gathered in my name, there am I" — Matt. 18:20).
Thank You, Lord. (Hold hands around the table as you give thanks.)

Bible Reading:

John 14:1-15

Questions

a. Verses 1-4. Where is Jesus going and why?

____

b. Verses 5-10. The disciples ask Him questions. Find the answers and put them in your own words. Jesus Himself is the way to ___

____

c. Verses 11-15. What "works" does Jesus want to do because He lives in us? ______.

Evening:

My prayer: Keep your Bible open and look at the words you have just read. Pray silently and ask Him (v. 14) for something.
Your prayer: Do the same.
Our prayer: Pray aloud and thank Him for who He is, for the "I AM'S" you can remember.

To remember:

Touch is important. Let's hold hands during prayer and make a bridge without words. Physical contact is nonverbal communication. We say things to each other by touch.

Day 5: *I AM the Vine.*

To memorize: Write out John 15:9-12 on paper for each child. Ask them to memorize it during the next few days.

Morning: Jesus is here. (Awareness starts with mental concentration. Say it. Believe it.)
Thank You, Lord, for . . . . (Let everyone think of three things.)

Bible Reading:

John 15:1-17

Questions:

a. What is this fruit (commandment) Jesus speaks of? ________
b. What does the branch do to bear fruit?
c. What does the vine do?
d. Which are you? What should you do today?
e. Underline the verses you like best.

Evening:

My prayer: Tell Jesus why you liked that verse.
Your prayer: You do the same.
Our prayer: Pray for others by name, putting God's love all around them.

To remember:

All the Ten Commandments are put into two simple ones by Jesus: Love God and love your neighbor. Here Jesus shows us how: Be a branch in the Vine.

Day 6: *I AM the Resurrection and the Life*

To Do: Review all the verses you have learned in this study and use some of them in the "thank you" time.

Morning: Jesus is here. (This starts the day off right!) Thank You, Lord. (We are forming the habit of being thankful.)

Bible Reading:

John 11:1-45

Questions:

a. What do you think "resurrection" means?
b. How do you think Lazarus felt?
c. How did Mary and Martha feel?
d. What did the others in the crowd think?

Evening:

My prayer: Whatever you feel and need.
Your prayer: Each one prays and responds with simplicity and honesty.
Our prayer: For others. Always surround them with God's love and yours, like a cloud.

To remember:

The more you know about Jesus, the more you will love Him.

Day 7: *I AM who I AM*

Morning: Jesus is here.
Thank You, Lord.

Bible Reading:

Exodus 3:14

Questions:

a. What was God's name?

____

b. John 8:58,59. What name does Jesus give to Himself?

____

c. John 8:23-30. Jesus knew who He was. What does He call Himself here?

____

d. What names of Jesus can you remember from our other lessons?

____

Evening:

My prayer and your prayer: By this time, your family should have the pattern established: anyone can start, then we respond or answer him, and then we pray our own request.

Our prayer: Pray for our nation, our president, and all the men and women in government offices.

To remember:

To know Him was to know God. John 10:14-15
To see Him was to see God. John 14:9
To believe in Him was to believe in God. John 14:1
To hate Him was to hate God. John 5:23
To honor Him was to honor God. John 5:23[1]

THIRD WEEK

Subject of the week: Precious Promises from God

Comments: God wants us to know how much He loves and cares about us, but we have an enemy who tries to make us forget. We should memorize these precious promises so they will be in our minds at the time of our need.

1st day: God is in everything that happens.
2nd day: Do not worry or be anxious.
3rd day: Your Father knows all your needs.
4th day: Precious promises for times of temptation.
5th day: God promises us anything, if. . . .
6th day: Precious promises for those who honor their parents.
7th day: God promises us life after death.

To remember:

There is not one perfect person in this world, but all of us are persons whom God loves. His precious promises are waiting for us to claim — waiting for us to use in time of need. Write the promise verses out on small cards and carry them around with you. Memorize them. Think about them. Use them. Believe them. Repeat them to others. God's precious promises are like a rock under our feet. All praise be to His name!

Day 1: *God is in everything that happens.*

Morning:

Jesus is here.
Thank You, Lord.

Bible Reading

Romans 8:28 (LB). "And we know that all that happens to us is working for our good if we love God and are fitting into his plans."

Philippians 2:13 (LB). "For God is at work within you, helping you want to obey him, and then helping you do what he wants.

1. What do you do when something bad happens? Like an accident, a quarrel, or temptation; when a pet dies, you have a disappointment, you lose a game, etc? Do you complain? Do you blame someone else?
2. Our first reaction when something happens is to blame someone or something. We must remember that in this world there is always an unseen conflict — a force trying to pull us away from Jesus, trying to make us forget to reach out to Him for help. We must call upon Him always.
3. Read those verses again. The first thing to do when something happens is to start thanking God and praising Him, because *He is in control.*

Evening:

Your prayer and my prayer:	Let us tell Jesus we trust Him, even in this difficult thing. Let us find something for which to thank Him.
Our prayer:	For others who may be in worse trouble than we are.

To remember:

No matter what happened, no matter whose fault it was, God loves you and will work it out for your good. Be patient. Give Him time. And give Him thanks.

Day 2: *Do not worry or be anxious.*

Morning: Jesus is here!
Thank You, Lord!

Bible Reading:

Philippians 4:6,7,13 (GN). "Don't worry about anything, but in all your prayers ask God for what you need, always asking him with a thankful heart. And God's peace, which is far beyond human understanding, will keep your hearts and minds safe, in Christ Jesus. . . . I have the strength to face all conditions by the power that Christ gives me."

John 14:27 (LB). "I am leaving you with a gift — peace of mind and heart! And the peace I give isn't fragile like the peace the world gives! So don't be troubled or afraid."

1. Something might happen. Or you are afraid something has happened. You pray hard: "Lord, take it away, make it go away." Wrong! Instead, pray, "Lord, I give it to You! You take over."
2. Here's the way I do it: I first tell Jesus all about it, how badly I feel, how dumb I am, how hurt, or how anxious. Then I tell Him what *I think* He ought to do, and then I turn around and give it up. Yes, I give it all to Him and pray, "Lord, You do whatever *You* know is best. I am Yours. I trust You."

Evening:

My prayer:	Tell Jesus all about it.
Your prayer:	Assure me that Jesus knows and hears. Pray the same for yourself, and I will respond and pray for you.
Our prayer:	For anyone concerned in the situation.

To remember:

A child in tears belongs in the Father's arms.
The cure for worry is giving thanks.

Day 3: *Your Father knows all your needs.*

Morning: Jesus is here. (Amazing fact.)
Thank You, Lord.

Bible Reading:

Matthew 6:32b,33,34 (LB) Your Father in heaven knows that you need all these things. So don't start worrying! Instead, give first place to His kingdom and to what He requires, and He will provide you with all these other things. Do not worry about tomorrow. (Read Matthew 6:25-34.)

Philippians 4:19 (LB). "And it is he who will supply all your needs from his riches in glory, because of what Christ Jesus has done for us."

a. "*His kingdom*" means doing His will and His work.
b. "*All these things*" means that nothing is too small to bring to your Father. If you need a postage stamp, ask Him.
c. "*Do not worry*" means giving thanks to your Father who cares.

Evening:

Your prayer and my prayer:	Your prayer and mine should be about the verses in today's reading.
Our prayer:	Our prayer should be for those we love who are not present.

To remember:

While we are in the act of prayer, let us try to remember to speak to Jesus from the child in our hearts, not the adult-person we seem to be.

Day 4: *Precious promises for times of temptation.*

Morning: Jesus is here!
Thank You, Lord!

Bible Reading:

Romans 8:24-29; 1 Corinthians 10:13 (LB). James 1:2,3 (LB). "Dear brothers, is your life full of difficulties and temptations? Then be happy, for when the way is rough, your patience has a chance to grow."

Romans 8:31,32 (LB). "What can we ever say to such wonderful things as these? If God is on our side, who can ever be against us?"

1. Temptation is in your mind; it is not an act.
2. If you keep on thinking about it, you may find yourself doing it.
3. Call on Jesus at once. Say His name, for He is powerful. When He is present, all is well.
4. If you fall (and we all do sometimes), God will forgive you (1 John 1:7).

Evening:

Your prayer and my prayer:	Let us confess our needs to Jesus and pray for one another. Then let us pray for others as the Holy Spirit leads us.
Our prayer:	(He will put the names of people we should pray for in our hearts and minds.)

To remember:

Turn back to chapter nine on the *Healing of Confession* and read through it again.

Instant confession restores the fellowship.

Day 5: *God promises us anything, if. . . .*

Comments: There is always an *if*, which means there is a cause and an effect in whatever happens. If I do so-and-so, then a certain thing will happen. (Example: if I turn on the faucet in the kitchen sink, the water will come.) The same is true of God's precious promises. We each have our part to do to make them work: God does His part, and I do mine.

Morning: Jesus is here!
Thank You, Lord!

Bible Reading:

Matthew 21:22 (LB). "You can get anything — *anything* you ask for in prayer — if you believe."

John 15:7,12 (LB, GN). "But if you stay in me and obey my commands, you may ask any request you like, and it will be granted. . . . This is my commandment: love one another, just as I love you."

1. Take a pencil and circle each *if* in the above verses.
2. Find what Jesus promises to do and what you and I must do to make the promises come true.
3. Why doesn't Jesus take away all the *ifs?* Because, when you do your own thing, it is hard to hear His voice. When you do His will,

your ears are open and you can hear better. At least, that is the way it works for me.

4. What shall we ask? When your ears are open, you can sometimes hear a voice (almost) inside you telling you *whom* to pray for and *what* to ask. When I ask without listening to Jesus, I usually don't want it after I get it! He knows better than I do what I really want or need. I'm learning to trust His love and wisdom.

Evening:

Prayer time: Follow the instructions in this lesson.

To remember:

Love opens all closed doors.
Love gives freely, but sometimes withholds.
God's timing is always right.

Day 6: *Precious promises for those who honor their parents.*

Bible Reading:

Ephesians 6:3 (LB). "And this is the promise: that if you honor your father and mother, yours will be a long life, full of blessing."

1. How can I honor my parents when they drink and mistreat us and each other?
   Answer: Jesus loves all sinners, but He does not love what they do. We must obey and honor the real person which is *inside* our parent, just as Jesus does. We should love and pray for them.
2. My parents demand perfection, and they make all my decisions for me. I'm not allowed to fail or to learn anything the hard way — so I'm afraid to fail.

Parents:

Discipline is one thing, but domination is another. Discipline allows for mistakes with guidance, and the children will respond to this. However, domination usually results in hostility (open or hidden) and stunts the development of personality. Hostility can be dissolved by just and fair discipline coupled with love and family prayers. Give your child the benefit of the good mind he has inherited from you, and let him learn to choose and decide at an early age. Only then can he be a person in his own right.

Love and pray for your children, and do not worry about them bringing disgrace on the family name. God is for you and with you. And that child is more important than what the neighbors think!

Children:

Hebrews 12:11 (LB). "Being punished isn't enjoyable while it is happening — it hurts! But afterwards we can see the result, a quiet growth in grace and character."

Evening:

Prayer time: This is a good time for honesty and forgiveness — for saying, *I love you* and *I'm sorry.*

To remember:

"Parents, do not treat your children in such a way as to make them angry. Instead, raise them with Christian discipline and instruction" (Eph. 6:4, GN).

Day 7: *God promises us life after death.*

Comments: Some people say this life is all there is, but Jesus came to tell us the truth. Read what He said.

Morning: Jesus is here!
Thank You, Lord!

Bible Reading

John 11:25 (LB). Jesus told her (Martha), "I am the one who raises the dead and gives them life again. Anyone who believes in me, even though he dies like anyone else, shall live again." (Also read v. 26.)

John 14:2,3 (LB). "There are many homes up there where my Father lives, and I am going to prepare them for your coming. When everything is ready, then I will come and get you."

1. What promise does Jesus give us today?
2. What does He do? What do we do?
3. Where does the Father live? What is He doing?
4. What will Jesus do when everything is ready?

Evening:

Prayer time: Pray for specific needs. Give thanks for special blessings.

To remember:

Those who suffer are the first to find their way to the heart of God.

FOURTH WEEK

Subject of the week: Praying Through the Psalms

Comments: Most of the Psalms were written by David, king of Israel, on four subjects: prayer, praise, prophecy, and meditation. The Psalms contain strong emotions and speak for us. They thunder about despair and death, roaring lions, wrath and glory, hills that clap their hands in joy, foundations of the world, chariots of war, wings of wind, angels and shepherds.[1]

The Psalms help us open our hearts and minds to God's love and nearness and His desire to meet our needs. In most of the books of the Bible, God is speaking to man; but in the Psalms, it is mostly man speaking to God.

This week we are going to learn how to make the Psalms our prayer book and pray our way through them by using David's words, adding our own words to them when we pray.

1st day: Psalm 1 The Way of Joy.
2nd day: Psalm 15 The Question and the Answer.
3rd day: Psalm 19 Our Great God.
4th day: Psalm 23 The Good Shepherd.
5th day: Psalm 24 The King of Glory.
6th day: Psalm 27 My Favorite Psalm.
7th day: My Prayer and God's Voice.

The book of Psalms is quoted 116 times in the New Testament by Jesus and other writers. It is the first prayer book of the believer. From the Psalms we learn words with which to give praise to God and words with which to confess our sins (Psalms 32 and 51). Please use a pen or sharp pencil to mark your Bible and a stiff card or bookmark to make straight lines. Mark the verses which "speak" to you, for that is the voice of God.

Day 1: *Psalm 1. The Way of Joy*

Morning: Jesus is here!
Thank You, Lord!

Bible Reading

1. Read Psalm 1 through from *The Living Bible.*
2. Find the two paths or ways and all the things that go with each way.
3. Can you suggest a new title?

Evening:

My prayer: With my Bible open to Psalm 1, use those words for making my own prayer and adding any I wish.
Your prayer: You do the same.
Our prayer: For all God's children in all nations.

To remember:

The Jesus prayer:
Lord Jesus Christ, Son of the living God,
have mercy on me, a sinner.

Day 2: *Psalm 15. The Question and The Answer*

Morning: Jesus is Here!
Thank You, Lord!

Bible Reading

1. Read Psalm 15 in *The Living Bible.*
2. Find the question and the answer.
3. Name some people you know who do these things. Thank God for them.
4. What is our "holy hill" today?

Evening:

Your prayer: With open Bible, tell the Lord what you need and what you can't do for yourself. Ask Him to do it.

My prayer: I'll respond to you and also use Psalm 15 to make my prayer.

Our prayer: Let us pray for all in prisons of any kind: for God's mercy, for light in their darkness.

To remember:

Next to lack of faith, the greatest barrier to answered prayer is lack of forgiveness. Let us not criticize those who fail, but let us pray for a forgiving spirit.

Day 3: *Psalm 19.*
Our Great God

Morning: Jesus is Here!
Thank You, Lord!

Bible Reading:

1. Read Psalm 19 in *The Living Bible.*
2. Read it aloud in unison if everyone has the same version.
3. vv. 1-6. God's glory shown in the ______.
   vv. 7-11. God's ways shown in the ______.
   vv. 12,13. God shows me my ________.

Evening:

Your prayer: With your Bible open, give praise to God for things He has made.

My prayer: I will join in with you as we think of things together, like a conversation.

Our prayer: For young people all over the world, that they may come to know Jesus as their personal Savior. For young people you know personally, that they might be filled and led by God's Holy Spirit in life's choices.

Day 4: *Psalm 23. The Good Shepherd*

Morning: Jesus Is Here!
Thank You, Lord!

Bible Reading

1. Read the 23rd Psalm aloud together.
2. How many names of the Shepherd can you remember?
3. What does He give the sheep?
4. Where does He take them?
5. What kind of a sheep are you?

Evening:

My prayer and your prayer: Turn to John 10:27-30. With your eyes on the words, use them to talk to Jesus about yourself and about Him.

Our prayer: Whatever is on our hearts, let us talk together with Jesus.

To remember:

A lost sheep belongs in the arms of the Shepherd.

Day 5: *Psalm 24. The King of Glory*

Morning: Jesus is here!
Thank You, Lord!
Good morning, Lord. What are You up to today? I'd like to be part of it.

> *Bible Reading*
>
> 1. Read Psalm 24 aloud. Then read it silently.
> 2. What does it tell you about yourself?
> 3. Find three questions starting with *who*. Find the answers.
> 4. What does this psalm teach us about God?

Evening:

Prayer time: Today our prayers should be filled with short praises to God. "Praise be to You, Lord God!" "Praise to You, Lord Jesus Christ!"

For more praises: Read the first verse only of Psalms 144—149. Read all of Psalm 150.

To remember:

Giving thanks is one thing. Giving praise is another. We thank God for His gifts to us. We praise Him for who He is. This is pure worship.

Day 6: *Psalm 27. My Favorite Psalm*

Morning: Jesus is Here!
Thank You, Lord!

Bible Reading

1. Read the psalm as if it were your prayer book.
2. Read verses 1-6. Stop any place you wish and tell God how you feel about Him. Then continue reading.
3. Verses 7-13. Just talk to the Lord, using these words, and adding your own. *Like v. 9.* "Oh, do not hide yourself when I am trying to find you" (LB). "Lord, I feel like that sometimes, for you seem so far away; but I know you don't really hide yourself — it just seems like it. I know you won't leave me now, for Jesus promised to always be with me, and I believe Him."
4. Go through all the verses like this, one by one. Verse 14 is one of the secrets of being a Christian.
5. Other passages to read: Romans 8:31; Isaiah 40:27-31.

Evening:

Prayer time: You have been having prayer time while your Bible reading was going on. You can pray back-and-forth as you wish, like a conversation, using the same verse.

Day 7: *John 17. My Prayer and God's Voice*

This is the last day of this series.
I know you will want to continue your reading.
My suggestion is that you turn back and read the psalms which we missed. Take them one at a time.

How to read these psalms:
Think about what you are reading.
Mark the verses which "speak" to you.
Pray through them, verse by verse.
God has many things to say to you.
Ask yourself, "What kind of a psalm is this?"

Here are a few examples, showing what "kind" they are:
Psalm 32 and 51 — confession of sins.
Psalm 34 — how close God is to His people.
Psalm 63 — searching for God.
Psalm 84 — a single day with the Lord.
Psalm 91 — His angels watch over us.
Psalm 103 — God's tender mercies and blessings.
Psalm 119 — all about God's wonderful laws.
Many of the last psalms are pure praise.

Problem:
What to do with *enemies* mentioned so often. See Psalm 30:1 and 31:1. The Old Testament has one idea about enemies (which we won't go into here), but Jesus taught us to love and pray for our enemies. I seldom have any enemies in person, so I put my own meaning on that word. My "enemies"

are the wrong feelings inside me which want to go my own way, instead of going God's way. Jesus is Victor! He can put down all the enemies within me and give me a heart to obey Him and to do His will. He can do that for you, too.

Bible Reading

The last assignment in the book on family prayer is to turn to the Gospel of John and read the seventeenth chapter. That is the wonderful last prayer of our Lord Jesus for all of us here and now. I know you will love it just as I do.

> "O holy Father! Keep them safe by the power of your name, the name you gave me, so they may be one just as you and I are one. . . . I made you known to them and I will continue to do so, in order that the love you have for me may be in them, and I may be in them."
>
> John 17:11,26 (GN)

Chapter Notes

Chapter 1

[1]"This constant moving creates a strain on the marriage. With this strain is the feeling of a lack of commitment and no sense of belonging to a community. This puts a responsibility on the family unit to satisfy its emotional needs. Often the family cannot meet that stress and pressure." Ken Olson, *The Art of Hanging Loose in an Uptight World* (Greenwich, CT: Fawcett Publications, Inc., 1974), p. 129.

Chapter 2

[1]Morton T. Kelsey, *The Art of Christian Love* (Pecos, NM: Dove Publications, 1975), pp. 5, 11.

Chapter 3

[1]Larry Christenson, *Which Way the Family?* (Minneapolis: Bethany Fellowship, 1973), pp. 3, 4.

[2]Ibid., pp. 8-11.

[3]Rosalind Rinker, *Prayer — Conversation With God* ("When the Family Prays Together"). Set of two cassettes available from Magnamedia, 17865 Park Circle, Irvine, CA 92714. $8.25 per set.

[4]Hope MacDonald, *Discovering How to Pray* (Grand Rapids: Zondervan Publishing House, 1976), pp. 14, 15.

Chapter 4

[1]David Geraets, O.S.B., *Jesus Beads* (Pecos, NM: Dove Publications).

[2]Rinker, *Praying Together* (Grand Rapids: Zondervan Publishing House, 1968), pp. 35-56.

[3]Harold H. Bloomfield, M.D.,*TM — Discovering Inner Energy and Overcoming Stress* (New York: Dell Publishing Co., 1976), back cover.

[4]Evelyn Underhill, *The Mount of Purification* (New York: Longmans, 1960), pp. 165, 169.

[5]M. V. Dunlop, *Introduction to Christian Meditation* (London: Billings & Sons, Ltd., 1963), pp. 32, 33.

[6]Brad Darrach, Review of *The Light at the Center: Context and Pretext of Modern Mysticism* by Agehananda Bharati, *Time* magazine (13 September 1976): 76, E9-11.
[7]George A. Maloney, *The Jesus Prayer* (Pecos, NM: Dove Publications, 1974).

Chapter 7

[1]Rinker, *God Loves You.* Two-pack cassette available from Magnamedia, Inc., 17865 Sky Park Circle, Suite H, Irvine, CA 92714.
[2]Rinker, *Meditation & Prayer Cards.* Available from Rosalind Rinker, c/o Zondervan Publishing House, 1415 Lake Drive, SE, Grand Rapids, MI 49506. $2.00 per hundred.

Chapter 9

[1]Rinker, *When the Family Prays Together.* (One of a series of six.) Available from Inspirational Tape Library, 5337 East Earll Drive, Phoenix, AZ 85018. $4.95 each. (Set of six available in two-pack cassette from Magnamedia, Inc., 17865 Sky Park Circle, Irvine, CA 92714. $8.95.)

Chapter 10

[1]Rinker, *Conversational Prayer* (Waco, TX: Word Books, 1976), pp. 86-95).
[2]Rinker, *Prayer: Conversing With God* (Grand Rapids: Zondervan, 1959). (Youth edition: *Praying Together,* 1968.)

Part III
Second week — 7th day

[1]John Stott, *Basic Christianity* (Grand Rapids: Eerdmans, 1957), p. 27.

Fourth week — Introduction

[1]Irving L. Jensen, *Psalms, a Self-study Guide* (Chicago: Moody Press, 1968).

Recommended Reading

FOR CHILDREN

Barrett, Ethel. *It Didn't Just Happen.* Glendale, CA: Regal Books, 1967. Devotional Bible stories.

Fletcher, Sarah. *Prayers for Little People.* St. Louis, MO: Concordia Publishing House, 1974.
Illustrated booklet — 79¢.

God Wants You. Glendale, CA: Gospel Light Publishers, 1974.
Series of small illustrated booklets — 45¢ each.

Jahsmann, Allan H., and Simon, Martin P. *Little Visits With God.* St. Louis, MO: Concordia Publishing House, 1957.
Devotionals (200) for children from ages 4-10, paperback — $2.95.

———. *More Little Visits With God.* St. Louis, MO: Concordia Publishing House, 1961.
Devotionals similar to above — same price.

Lehn, Cornelia. *God Keeps His Promise.* Scottdale, PA: Herald Press, 1970.
A Bible storybook for kindergarten children.

Lewis, C. S. *Chronicles of Narnia.* New York: Macmillan Publishing Company, Inc., 1970
Seven fantasies where the characters portray spiritual truths, paperback — $1.25 each (also come in boxed set).

Taylor, Kenneth N. *Devotions for the Children's Hour.* Chicago, IL: Moody Press, 1954.

The ABC's of Proverbs. New York: American Bible Society.

Schreivogel, Paul A. *Small Prayers for Small Children About Big and Little Things.* Minneapolis, MN: Augsburg Publishing House, 1971.
I have a gift copy from the author — it's good!

FOR FAMILIES

Aaseng, Rolf E. *God Is Great, God Is Good: Devotions for Families.* Minneapolis, MN: Augsburg Publishing House, 1972.
Beautiful format. Each devotion has an opening sentence to start the discussion, then the story and teaching about God from the life

of Jesus and from the lives of Moses, David, Samuel, etc. Highly recommended. Fifty-six devotions for families with children from ages 3-11, cloth — $3.95.

Anson, Elva. *The Family That Prays Together.* Chicago, IL: Moody Press, 1975.
Full of ideas for family devotions for all ages, paper — $2.50.

Barkman, Frieda. *Look for the Wonder: A Family Celebrates Its Faith.* Glendale, CA: Regal Books, 1975.
Stories that show how a family brings God into everything, paper — $1.45.

Graded Daily Bible Reading Material. Scripture Union, 1716 Spruce Street, Philadelphia, PA 19103.
Material for ages 3-6, 7-10, 11-14, high school, and several adult booklets varying in depth and content. I recommend this series and urge you to send for their sample publications catalog.

Haskin, Dorothy C. *God in My Family.* Anderson, IN: Warner Press Publishers, 1970. Devotions for 30 days.

Schaeffer, Francis and Edith. *Everybody Can Know.* Wheaton, IL: Tyndale House Publishers, 1975.
An exciting adventure from the Gospel of Luke. Effective when read aloud. For ages 6-18, cloth — $6.95.

Ulrich, Betty G. *Every Day With God: Devotions for Families With Children.*
Fifty stories about everyday living situations, paper — $3.50.

FOR PARENTS

Beardsley, Lou. *A Family Love Story.* Irvine, CA: Harvest House Publications, Inc., 1976.
A book of real-life family situations to help you recognize your own situations, paper — $2.95.

Christenson, Larry. *The Christian Family.* Minneapolis, MN: Bethany Fellowship, Inc., 1970.
Guidelines for developing as Christians in the family.

———. *Which Way the Family?* Minneapolis, MN: Bethany Fellowship, Inc., 1973.
Practical, down-to-earth help for families, paper booklet — 50¢.

Elliott, Norman K. *God Really Loves You.* St. Paul, MN: Macalester Park Publishing Co., 1954.
Booklet — 3 for $1.00.

Kelsey, Morton T. *The Art of Christian Love.* Pecos, NM: Dove Publications, 1975.
Short studies of the many facets of love, booklet — 65¢.

Kesler, Jay. *Living in Love.* Youth for Christ International.
A guide to effective adult-teen relationships.

MacDonald, Hope. *Discovering How to Pray.* Grand Rapids, MI: Zondervan Publishing House, 1976.
A new book I recommend, paper — $1.75.

Rinker, Rosalind. *Who Is This Man?* Grand Rapids, MI: Zondervan Publishing House, 1960.
Studies in the Gospel of Mark, paper — $1.50.

———. *Prayer: Conversing With God.* Grand Rapids, MI: Zondervan Publishing House, 1959.
A classic on prayer, paper — $1.25.

———. *Conversational Prayer.* Waco, TX: Word, Inc., 1970.
Teacher's handbook, paper — $2.50.

BIBLES

New International Version New Testament. Grand Rapids, MI: Zondervan Bible Publishers, 1973.
Available in several formats, varying in price.

New International Version New Testament, Children's Edition. Grand Rapids, MI: Zondervan Bible Publishers, 1975.
Beautiful children's edition of NIV for pre-school through sub-teen. Includes illustrated Bible dictionary, exclusive Memory Margin,™ thirty original color illustrations, and many other study aids — $7.95.

The Bible in Pictures for Little Eyes. Wheaton, IL: Tyndale House Publishers.
Full-color illustrations (190) and simple text, cloth — $4.95.

The Children's Living Bible. Wheaton, IL: Tyndale House Publishers.
Children's edition of the Kenneth Taylor paraphrase with Hook illustrations — $4.95.

The Way (Living Bible) Catholic Edition. Wheaton IL: Tyndale House Publishers.
Vinyl cover, handbook size, photographs — $5.95.

CASSETTES

Rinker, Rosalind. *When the Family Prays Together.* One of a series of six — $4.95 each. Inspirational Tape Library, 5337 East Earll Drive, Phoenix, AZ 85018. Set of six available from Magnamedia, Inc., 17865 Sky Park Circle, Irvine, CA 92714.